C. C. Cline

Standard Sunday-school hymnal

C. C. Cline

Standard Sunday-school hymnal

ISBN/EAN: 9783337089962

Printed in Europe, USA, Canada, Australia, Japan

Cover: Foto ©Thomas Meinert / pixelio.de

More available books at **www.hansebooks.com**

THE STANDARD SUNDAY-SCHOOL HYMNAL

COMPILED AND EDITED BY

C. C. CLINE

COMPILER OF POPULAR HYMNS, THE STANDARD CHURCH HYMNAL, ETC.

CINCINNATI
THE STANDARD PUBLISHING COMPANY
16 TO 20 EAST NINTH STREET

CONTENTS.

THE LIFE OF JESUS,	1– 59
LOVING AND PRAISING,	65–101
WORKING FOR JESUS,	105–151
THE WORDS OF JESUS,	155–170
TEMPERANCE SONGS,	175–215
NATURE'S MELODIES,	220–233
HOME AND HEAVEN,	240–265
INFANT CLASS,	270–321
MISCELLANEOUS,	325-343

THE LIFE OF JESUS.

"As long as I am in the world, I am the Light of the world."—Jno. 9: 5

Star of the Morning.

"I am the root of David, the bright and morning star."—Rev. 22: 16.

Rev. W. F. Cosner.   R. A. Glenn.

1. Rise in thy splendor, O star of the morning, Let the bright beams of thy glo-ry ap-pear; Light of the world, bring us out of the darkness, Gra-cious-ly keep us when dan-ger is near. Rise in thy splen - dor, O beau-ti-ful star, . . . Let the bright rays . . . of thy glo-ry ap-pear, Shine in our hearts, . . . bring com-fort and peace, . . . When thou art near us our sor-row shall cease.

2 Rise in thy splendor, O star of the morning,
  Shine in our hearts, bring us comfort and peace;
  Jesus, Redeemer, our hope and salvation,
    When thou art near us our sorrow shall cease.

3 Rise in thy splendor, O star of the morning,
  Beautiful morn-star by prophets foretold;
  "Light of the world," fill the earth with thy glory
    May we the "King in his beauty behold."

Copyright, 1885, by R. A. Glenn.

The Shepherds of Bethlehem.

"There were ... shepherds ... keeping watch over their flocks by night"—LUKE 2: 8.

B. R. HANBY.

1. They were watch-ing on the hill-sides for the com-ing day, With the star-ry folds of night a-bove them spread, When a glo-ry flashed a-round them, shin-ing rays Thro' the pearl-y por-tals on them shed.

CHORUS. Faster, and with energy.

"Glo-ry to God in the high-est!" Came float-ing down the air; "Glo-ry to God in the high-est!" Seemed ring-ing ev-'ry-where; Glo-ry, glo-ry, O chil-dren, Come, sing that song a-gain. "Glo-ry to God in the high-est, Good-will and peace to men."

Used by permission of The John Church Co., owners of the Copyright.

2 Louder swell the joyful anthems from the angel throng;
Over hill and vale the strains enchanted float;
See the wond'ring shepherds list'ning to the song,
Trembling, yet rejoicing at the sight.

3 O the joyful, joyful tidings! for to you is Christ
Born, the wondrous Saviour and the mighty King;
Hail, ye waiting nations, hail this joyous morn!
Happy tidings now to earth we bring.

3. Good Tidings of Great Joy.

TATE AND BRADY. GEORGE FREDERICK HANDEL.

1. While shep-herds watched their flocks by night, All seat-ed on the ground, The an-gel of the Lord came down, And glo-ry shone a-round, And glo-ry shone a-round.

2 "Fear not," said he,—for mighty dread
Had seized their troubled mind,—
"Glad tidings of great joy I bring,
To you and all mankind.

3 "To you, in David's town, this day
Is born, of David's line,
The Saviour, who is Christ the Lord;
And this shall be the sign:

4 "The heavenly babe you there shall find
To human view displayed,

All meanly wrapped in swathing-bands,
And in a manger laid."

5 Thus spake the seraph; and forthwith
Appeared a shining throng
Of angels, praising God on high,
Who thus addressed their song:

6 "All glory be to God on high,
And to the earth be peace:
Good-will henceforth from heaven to men,
Begin and never cease."

4. Silent Night.

Words from the German. GERMAN AIR.

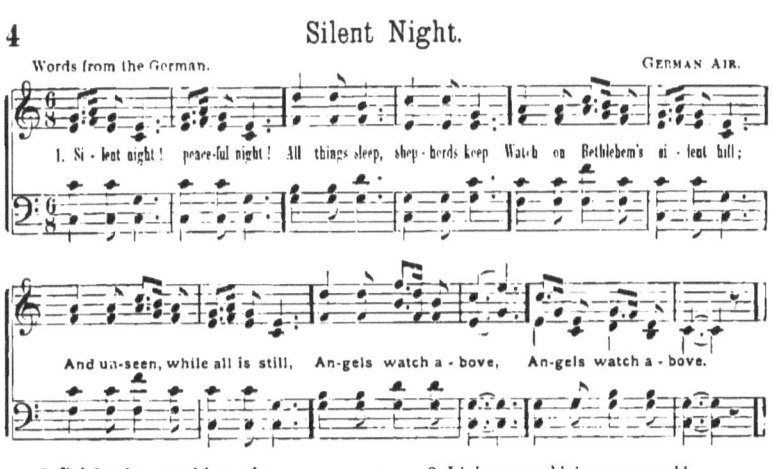

1. Si-lent night! peace-ful night! All things sleep, shep-herds keep Watch on Bethlehem's si-lent hill; And un-seen, while all is still, An-gels watch a-bove, An-gels watch a-bove.

2 Bright the star shines afar,
Guiding trav'lers on their way;
Who their gold and incense bring,
Off'rings to the promised King,
Child of David's line.

3 Light around! joyous sound!
Angel voices wake the air;
Glory be to God in heaven,
Peace on earth to you is given;
Lo! the Christ is born!

5. The King in the Manger.

"Ye shall find the babe wrapped in swaddling clothes lying in the manger."—LUKE 2: 12.

DR. J. G. HOLLAND.   R. M. McINTOSH, by per.

2 There's a tumult of joy o'er the wonderful birth,
  For the Virgin's sweet boy is the Lord of the earth.
  CHO.—Ay, the star rains its fire, while the Beautiful sing,
    For the manger of Bethlehem cradles a King, etc.

3 In the light of that star lie the ages impearled,
  And that song from afar has swept over the world.
  CHO.—Every heart is aflame, while the Beautiful sing,
    In the homes of the nations, that Jesus is King, etc.

4 We rejoice in the light, and we echo the song
  That comes down through the night from the heavenly throng.
  CHO.—Ay, we shout to the lovely evangel they bring,
    And we greet in his cradle our Saviour and King, etc.

6. Who is This?

"Who is this that cometh from Edom, with dyed garments from Bozrah?"—Is. 63: 1.

ANON   E. S. LORENZ.

Used by permission of E. S. Lorenz, owner of the Copyright.

7. Brightest and Best.

FABER. "Thine eyes shall see the King in his beauty." — Is. 33: 17. E. S. LORENZ.

2 Cold on his mantle the dewdrops are shining,
   Low lies his head with the beasts of the stall;
  Angels adore him in slumber reclining,
   Maker and Monarch and Saviour of all.
3 Say, shall we yield him, in costly devotion,
   Odors of Eden and off'rings divine?

Gems of the mountain and pearls of the ocean,
 Myrrh from the forest or gold from the mine?
4 Vainly we offer each ample oblation,
 Vainly with gold would his favor secure;
 Richer by far is the heart's adoration,
 Dearer to God are the prayers of the poor.

Who is This? Concluded.

2 Who is this, a man of sorrows,
   Walking sadly life's hard way?
  Homeless, weary, sighing, weeping
   Over sin and Satan's sway?
  'Tis our God, our glorious Saviour,
   Who above the starry sky
  Now prepares the many mansions
   Where no tear can dim the eye.
3 Who is this, behold him shedding
   Drops of blood upon the ground?
  Who is this—despised, rejected,
   Mocked, insulted, beaten, bound?

'Tis our God, who gifts and graces
 On his church now poureth down;
Who shall smite in holy vengeance
 All his foes beneath his throne.
4 Who is this that hangeth dying,
 While the rude world scoffs and scorns?
On the cross with sinners numbered,
 Pierced by nails and crowned with thorns?
'Tis the God who ever liveth
 'Mid the shining ones on high,
In the glorious golden city,
 Reigning everlastingly.

8. Beautiful Star In The East.

HARRIET E. JONES. FRANK M. DAVIS, by per.

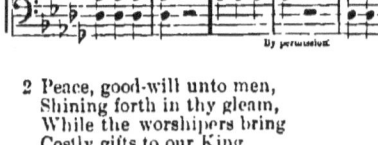

1. There's a star in the East, There are songs in the air, There is joy in the earth O'er the wonderful birth Of Mes-si-ah, the Savior and Heir; Of Mes-si-ah, the Savior and Heir.

CHORUS.
Star . . . in the East, . . . Star . . . in the East, . . . In thy grandeur shine on o'er the Infinite One, Star . . . in the East; . . . Star . . . in the East, . . . Beau-ti-ful star in the East.

Beau-ti-ful star, star in the East; Beau-ti-ful star, Star in the East, In thy grandeur shine on o'er the Infinite One, Beau-ti-ful star, Star in the East, Beau-ti-ful star, Star in the East, Beau-ti-ful star in the East, in the East.

By permission.

2 Peace, good-will unto men,
Shining forth in thy gleam,
While the worshipers bring
Costly gifts to our King
Who has graciously come to redeem;
Who has graciously come to redeem.

3 'Tis our Prophet and Priest,
Says the star in the East,
The Redeemer foretold
By the wise men of old,
And the tidings our joy has increased;
And the tidings our joy has increased.

9. In a Manger.

"The babe lying in a manger."—LUKE 2: 16.

VINNIE VERNON.   E. S. LORENZ.

1. In the ho-ly hush of twi-light, On that morn-ing long a-go, Bent the hosts of an-gels wond'ring, Gaz-ing on a scene be-low. In a man-ger, Lo! a stranger, Saw they ly-ing cra-dled low;

D. C. Prince of glo-ry, (Strange, strange sto-ry!) Was he ly-ing there so low?

Copyright, 1878, by E. S. LORENZ.

2 Silence held the court of Heaven,
Till the wonder found a voice,
In a sudden burst of rapture,
Waking mortals to rejoice.

3 Shepherds caught the shout of gladness,
As they watched the fleecy fold;
Wise men saw the star whose rising
Ancient prophets had foretold.

4 But of all who sang him welcome,
On that morning long ago,
None shall give him greater praises,
Than our hearts that love him so.

5 Hail to thee, dear infant Saviour,
Lord of heaven, Prince of peace!
Take our souls and reign within us,
Till all sin and strife shall cease.

10. Condescension.

"Though he was rich, yet for our sakes he became poor."

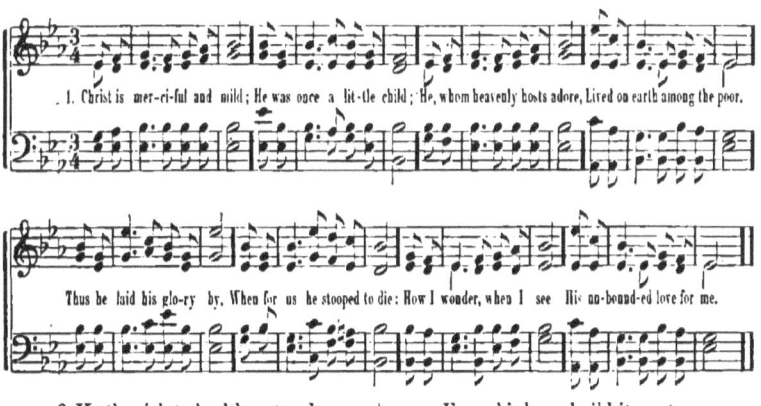

1. Christ is mer-ci-ful and mild; He was once a lit-tle child; He, whom heavenly hosts adore, Lived on earth among the poor. Thus he laid his glo-ry by, When for us he stooped to die; How I wonder, when I see His un-bound-ed love for me.

2 He the sick to health restored,
To the poor he preached the word;
Even children had a share
Of his love and tender care.

Every bird can build its nest;
Foxes have their place of rest;
He who our salvation made,
Had not where to lay his head.

11. O Watching Stars, Rejoice.

PRISCILLA J. OWENS.
FRANK M. DAVIS, by per.

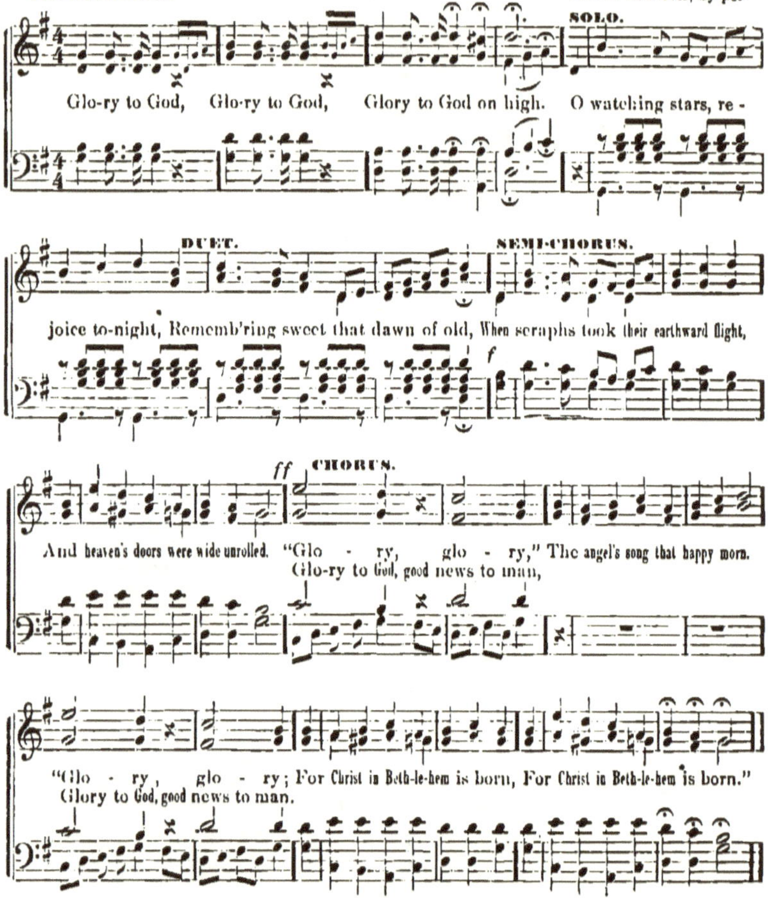

Glo-ry to God, Glo-ry to God, Glory to God on high. O watching stars, rejoice to-night, Rememb'ring sweet that dawn of old, When seraphs took their earthward flight, And heaven's doors were wide unrolled. "Glo - ry, glo - ry," The angel's song that happy morn. Glo-ry to God, good news to man, "Glo - ry, glo - ry; For Christ in Beth-le-hem is born, For Christ in Beth-le-hem is born." Glory to God, good news to man.

2 He came, sin's tyrant chain to break,
To bid the captive soul go free,
The mournful sleep of death to wake
With notes of heav'n's own jubilee.

3 Go, speed the joyous tidings forth,
Resounding far through distant time;
The grateful voices of the earth
Shall swell amid those tones sublime.

12. Who Among the Mighty?

F. M. D.
FRANK M. DAVIS.

Messiah comes! the mighty Saviour! Of all the kings is King: Let earth rejoice and give him honor, And loud his praises sing.

Who Among the Mighty? Concluded.

2 Then hail with joy the great Deliv'rer,
The mighty Prince of Peace;
The night of sin away is passing,
And strife on earth must cease.

3 Let every kindred, tribe, and nation
That's ransomed from the fall,
Raise high the song of adoration,
And crown him Lord of all.

13 Hark, to the Wondrous Music!

"For unto you is born this day in the city of David a Savior."—Luke 2: 11.

FRANK M. DAVIS.

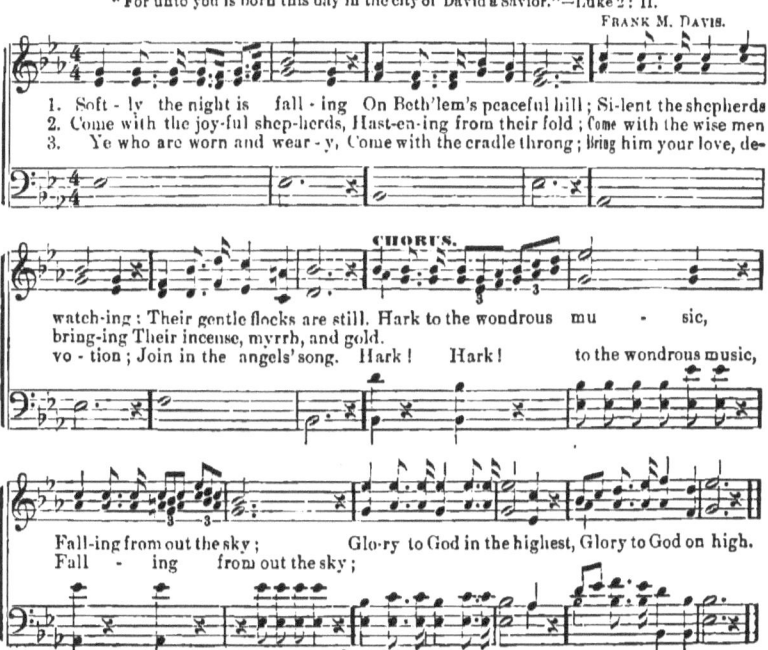

1. Soft - ly the night is fall - ing On Beth'lem's peaceful hill; Si-lent the shepherds watch-ing; Their gentle flocks are still. Hark to the wondrous music, Fall-ing from out the sky; Glory to God in the highest, Glory to God on high.
2. Come with the joy-ful shep-herds, Hast-en-ing from their fold; Come with the wise men bring-ing Their incense, myrrh, and gold. Hark! Hark! to the wondrous music, Fall - ing from out the sky;
3. Ye who are worn and wear - y, Come with the cradle throng; Bring him your love, de-vo - tion; Join in the angels' song.

14. Suffer Little Children.

Rev. John O. Foster, A. M.
Chas. H. Gabriel.

1 Suffer little children, so the Master said,
With his hands extended,
Gather round his altars, little ones to-day,
Singing songs of praises, learning how to pray.

2 Suffer little children, love to all extend,
Like the blessed Saviour, be their dearest friend,
Lead them to believe him, worship and obey,
Follow on to know him, in the living way.

3 Suffer little children, say to one and all:
Answer Jesus' welcome, listen to his call,
Run to him with gladness, you will surely know
He is ever ready righteousness to show.

4 Suffer little children, seek and you shall find
Hidden, costly treasures, jewels for the mind,
Crowns of fadeless glory, robes of purest white,
And the many mansions in the world of light.

15. He Came For Me.

Unknown.
Alex. C. Hopkins.

1 Jesus, my Saviour, in Bethlehem came,
Born in a manger to sorrow and shame;
O, it was wonderful, blest be his name,
Seeking for me, seeking for me.

2 Jesus, my Saviour, on Calvary's tree,
Paid the great debt and my soul he set free;
O, it was wonderful, how could it be?
Dying for me, dying for me.

3 Jesus, my Saviour, the same as of old,
While I did wander afar from the fold;
Gently and long he has plead with my soul,
Calling for me, calling for me.

4 Jesus, my Saviour, shall come from on high,
Sweet is the promise as weary years fly;
O, I shall see him descending the sky,
Coming for me, coming for me.

16 The Barren Fig-Tree.

Mrs. M. B. C. Slade. R. M. McIntosh, by per.

In the vineyard of the Master, There was growing once a tree, Thither came he often, hoping That some fruit thereon might be. Fruit, not blossom, went he seeking, Only leaves thereon he found; To his dresser hear him speaking, Lo, it cumbereth the ground.

CHORUS.
If the Master to our vineyard, Should this day come down, Seeking, looking, asking for his own. Ready for his eye are we? Is there fruit upon our tree? Will he bid the dresser cut it down?

2 But the dresser then made answer,
    Leave it, Lord, another year;
  I with care will tend and keep it,
    Till the bud and bloom appear,
  Then if ripened fruit be showing,
    It is well, my Lord will own,
  If but leaves are on it growing,
    After that, Lord, cut it down.

3 In the vineyard of my Master,
    Oft my tree his patience tries,
  Seeking fruit he often cometh,
    Finding only useless leaves.
  Let thy dews of grace fall on me,
    Till some fruits divine appear;
  Let thy patience rest upon me,
    Try me, Lord, another year.

17. Peace, Be Still!

Mrs. M. B. C. Slade. R. M. McIntosh, by per.

1. Rocked up-on the rag-ing bil-low, While the tem-pest tossed the deep, Calm-ly on the sea-man's pil-low, Je-sus lay in qui-et sleep, Wild-er grew the storm and fast-er; Soon the waves the ves-sel fill; Wake, they cry, we per-ish, Master! He can save us if he will. *CHORUS.* Sweet-ly hear the Sav-iour say-ing—Storm-y sea and tem-pest stay-ing, Wind and wa-ters all o-bey-ing, Hear him say-ing, "Peace, be still!"

2 Frightened, faithless, trembling, tearful,
Jesus kindly to them saith:
Why, O, why are ye so fearful?
How is it ye have no faith?
Lord, we perish, they are crying;
Save us, Lord, they pray, until,
Calm as softest zephyrs sighing,
Wind and sea obey his will.

3 When with sorrows o'er us breaking,
Or with sin's wild tempest tossed,
If we cry, the Master seeking,
Save us, Lord, or we are lost!
Neither wind nor sea shall harm us;
All obey the heavenly will;
If we trust him he will calm us;
Peace divine our souls shall fill.

18 Walking the Sea.

J. P. Ellis.   A. S. Kieffer, by per.

1. There's a light on the dark and surg-ing deep, That shines when the loud winds roar; And the form of the Friend who does not sleep, Comes on from the oth-er shore, Walk-ing the sea, ... to you and to me; Walk-ing the sea, Keep-ing the light of us, e'er to be-friend, Ev-er in sight of us, suc-cor to lend, Walk-ing the sea, ... Walk-ing the sea. Walk-ing the sea,

2 There's a light in the depths of surging life
That shineth for evermore;
And the Friend who would stay all sin and strife,
Is here from the other shore,
Walking life's sea, to you and to me;
Walking so carefully, seeking to find,
Ever so prayerfully, earnest and kind,
Walking the sea, walking the sea.

3 There's a light in the depths of Christian hearts,
That gleams on the crown before;
And the Saviour, whose love a bliss imparts,
Attends to the other shore,
Walking life's sea, with you and with me;
Keeping in reach of us, watching for all,
Caring for each of us, lest we should fall,
Walking the sea, walking the sea.

19. It is I, be not Afraid.

"Be of good cheer; it is I, be not afraid."—MATT. 14: 27.

I. BALTZELL. A S. KIEFFER, by per.

2 The storm could not bury that word in the wave,
'Twas taught through the tempest to fly;
It shall reach his disciples in every clime,
Saying, "Be not afraid, it is I."

3 When the spirit is broken with sorrow and care,
And comfort is ready to die;
Then the darkness shall pass, and the sunshine appear,
By the life-giving word, "It is I."

4 When death is at hand, and the cottage of clay
Is left with a tremulous sigh;
The gracious Redeemer will light all the way,
With the soul-cheering word, "It is I."

5 When the river is passed, and the glories unknown
Burst forth on the wondering eye,
He will welcome, encourage, and comfort his own,
Saying, "Be not afraid, it is I."

20. The Lilies of the Field.

"Consider the lilies of the field."—MATT. 6: 28.

W. O. PERKINS, by per.

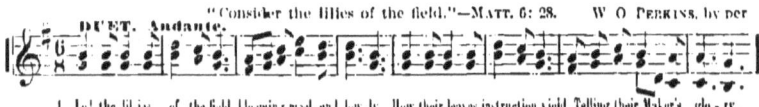

21. Jesus in the Vessel.

"Then they received him into the ship."   JAMES PRICE.

2 Though our way is dark and dreary,
And the wind is fierce and strong,
Though our hands grow faint and weary,
But the tempest won't be long,
We will sail through storm and danger,
Through the darkest clouds that form,
And with Jesus in the vessel,
We will smile at the storm.

3 O'er the dark and stormy ocean
We will sail at his command,
Bravely face the wild commotion,
Till we reach the better land.
Courage, then, come wind and weather,
Come the darkest clouds that form,
For with Jesus in the vessel
We will smile at the storm.

The Lilies of the Field. Concluded.

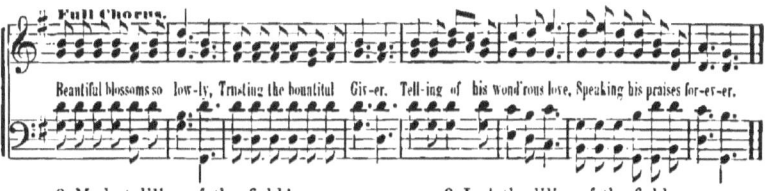

2 Modest lilies of the field!
When the rain-drops glisten,
How they nod their pretty heads,
Bending as if to listen!
So may I God's word receive,
Down in my heart so lowly;
Mourn my sin, and then believe
In the blest Saviour so holy.

3 Lo! the lilies of the field
Send up joy and brightness
From their sweet and fragrant leaves,
Perfect in all their whiteness.
Thus may I so live below,
That, when the angels greet me,
On the bright and shining shore,
Jesus may hasten to meet me.

22. Blue Sea of Galilee.

HARRIET E. JONES.   FRANK M. DAVIS.

By permission.

1 O wondrous sea of Galilee!
   In yonder land so bright and fair;
   O sweet to me the thoughts of thee,
   And One who loved to linger there.

2 Would I had been with Jesus there,
   In that dear nook beside the sea,
   His words of love my heart to move,
   And his sweet smile to gladden me.

3 O praise his name! he's just the same,
   As when he stood beside the sea;
   He answers prayer as he did there
   In that fair land of Galilee.

4 When storm-clouds dark are round my bark,
   While out upon life's troubled sea,
   He stills the waves and sweetly saves,
   Just as he did in Galilee.

23. Memories of Galilee.

1 Each cooing dove and sighing bough
   That makes the eve so blest to me,
   Has something far diviner now,
   It bears me back to Galilee.

CHO.—O Galilee! sweet Galilee!
   Where Jesus loved so much to be;
   O Galilee! blue Galilee!
   Come, sing thy song again to me!

2 Each flowery glen and mossy dell
   Where happy birds in song agree,
   Thro' sunny morn the praises tell
   Of sights and sounds in Galilee.—Cho.

3 And when I read the thrilling love
   Of him who walked upon the sea,
   I long, oh, how I long once more
   To follow him in Galilee.—Cho.

24. Thy Will Be Done.

Mrs. M. B. C. Slade. — Dr. A. B. Everett, by per.

2 Come down among the fishers, beside the shining lake,
   The blue and placid lake of Galilee,
   And hear how Jesus calleth, come now, your nets forsake;
   Then, leaving all, cry, Lord, we follow thee.

3 Come out into the desert, where Jesus went before,
   The cold and dreary, rocky wilderness;
   And learn how Jesus suffered, with temptings dark and sore,
   And there the Lord thy God, with him confess.

4 Come up into the garden, by Olive's mount of prayer,
   The place of tears and pain, Gethsemane;
   And, weeping, say with Jesus, as he is weeping there,
   Just as thou wilt, dear Lord, do unto me.

5 And can you follow Jesus, tho' pain and death draw nigh,
   By Calv'ry's way, up which the Saviour passed?
   And faithful in his service before him, by and by,
   Receive the blessed words, "well done," at last?

25. The Mustard Seed.

Mrs. M. B. C. Slade. Read Matt. xiii. 31, 32. R. M. McIntosh, by per.

Lik-en the kingdom to the springing, Springing of small-est seeds we know; Soon in the branch-es birds are sing-ing, So shall the heav'nly kingdom grow. Wide o'er the mead, Fling thou the seed, Sun-shine of heav-en shall be giv-en, Seed of the king-dom free-ly sow.

2 Say not, too humble seems thy planting,
Trust in the story Jesus told;
Dews of his grace our Lord is granting,
Soon shall it yield an hundred fold.

3 O! the rejoicing, when at even,
Thy labor ended, safe at home,
High in the branches, up in heaven
Singing, "O Lord, thy kingdom come!"

26. Blind Bartimeus.

"And Jesus said unto him, Go thy way; thy faith hath made thee whole."—Mark 10: 52.

M. B. C. Slade. R. M. McIntosh, by per.

1. As forth from the cit-y went Je-sus one day, They came to a blind man, who heard, by the way,
2. What wilt thou, said Je-sus, shall I do to thee? He answered him, Lord, that my eyes o-pened be;

'Tis Je-sus of Naz-a-reth, now pass-ing by: Then, though they rebuked, more and more would he cry:
The Lord had com-pas-sion, and touch-ing his eyes, Re-stored them, in an-swer to faith's earnest cries:

27. The Sower.

Mrs. M. B. C. Slade.   R. M. McIntosh, by per.

2 Hear now the Teacher say, God's word the seed;
Are ye the wayside ones, giving no heed?
Or of the stony ground, hearers, are ye!
Or of the thorny ground, choked utterly?
Or shall an hundred fold fruit gathered be?

3 Sow thou thy seed divine, Lord, all around!
O make this heart of mine good, fruitful ground!
Smile on the harvest, Lord! rich may it be,
When we an hundred fold gather for thee!
Jesus the story told, on Galilee.

Blind Bartimæus. Concluded.

3 Then all, when they saw it, to God gave the praise;
And glory to God, doth he gratefully raise;
Rejoicing the face of the Master to see,
Who pitying heard, when believing cried he.

4 Dear Lord, when in darkness and blindness we stray,
To thee will we cry when thou passest this way;
We'll hold not our peace, but beseech more and more,
Lord, let thy compassion and pity restore.

28. The Vineyard Gate.

Mrs. M. B. C. SLADE.   R. M. McIntosh, by per.

The Master stood at the vineyard gate, And early at morn-ing cried he: Oh, laborers, come, nor long-er wait, Come, work in my vine-yard for me. They toiled from morn till the day was past; The Lord then un-to them came, And gave to the first, and gave the last, As tho' they had labored the same.

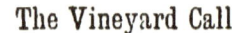

Copyright 1882, by R. M. McIntosh.

2 So, hour by hour, would he come and see
  The idlers, and unto them say:
My vineyard within go also ye,
  Why stand ye here idle all day?
And then when even was come he bade
  His steward all of them call,
And render to each his hire, he said,
  And equally give unto all.

3 The vineyard gate of our Lord Divine,
  O shall we not enter it now?
He needs us to tend each fruitful vine,
  His spirit is showing us how.
And when our labor is done below,
  As fall the shadows of night,
The Lord of us all is just, we know,
  He'll give us whatever is right.

29. The Vineyard Call.

Rev. F. A. HOFFMAN.   R. M. McIntosh, by per.

Hear the Master calling, for toilers calling, Oh! so loudly calling to you and me, Enter now in the vineyard and no long-er i-dle be, But for Je-sus la-bor faith-ful-ly.

REFRAIN.

He is call-ing,

The Lily of the Valley.

2 He all my griefs has taken, and all my sorrows borne,
   In temptation he's my strong and mighty tower;
   I have all for him forsaken, and all my idols torn
   From my heart, and now he keeps me in his power;
   Though all the world forsake me, and Satan tempts me sore,
   Through Jesus I shall safely reach the goal; He's the, etc.

3 He'll never, never leave me, nor yet forsake me here,
   While I live by faith and do his blessed will;
   A wall of fire about me, I've nothing now to fear;
   With his manna he my hungry soul shall fill;
   Then sweeping up to glory, to see his blessed face,
   Where rivers of delight shall ever roll; He's the, etc.

The Vineyard Call. Concluded.

2 He has long been calling, for workers calling,
   Oh! so gently calling and tenderly!
   And the hours have been speeding, quickly hastening away,
   And we've wasted all the precious day.

3 Jesus still is calling, for servants calling,
   In his love he's calling to you and me;
   Haste! the day is declining, and ere long it will be gone,
   And the dark and dreaded night come on!

31. Go Gather the Golden Grain.

J. CALVIN BUSHEY.

1 The fields are ripe with harvest,
  And the Master calls again:
  "Why stand here idly waiting?
  Go gather the golden grain!"

2 In youth's bright golden morning,
  Hear the Saviour's voice so plain:
  "If you love not one another,
  Who'll gather the golden grain?"

3 While suff'ring is around us,
  Shall the Master call in vain?
  Lending aid for fallen brothers,
  Is gathering golden grain.

4 If we would dwell in heaven
  With the holy angel train,
  We must labor in the vinyard,
  Must gather the Master's grain.

32. Galilee.

R. MORRIS, D. D., LL. D.   R. M. McINTOSH, by per.

33 The Marriage of the King's Son.

Mrs. M. B. C. Slade. R. M. McIntosh, by per.

Once a feast was made and the board was laid, And the king array'd in his garments fair;

For my son, said he, shall the glad feast be; Bear my message free; bid the guests be there.

CHORUS.

When for you and me such a call shall be, When the King cries come, shall we joyful rise and go?

Oh, rejoice, rejoice, for I hear his voice, To his feast we'll haste, for he loves us so.

2 Forth again he sent, and his servants went
  To the bidden guests, but they turned away;
  Then the king was wroth, and he hastened forth,
  And the sounds of wrath filled the festal day.

3 Once again he cried, for my feast supplied,
  From the highway side gather one and all,
  Lo, they quickly haste to the marriage feast,
  To each lowly guest 'tis a welcome call.

4 When our King shall call, may we one and all
  In his palace hall haste to take our seat;
  Wedding garments fair, love and grace prepare,
  We'll rejoicing wear, when the King we meet.

Galilee. Concluded.

2 Each flow'ry glen and mossy dell,
  Where happy birds in song agree,
  Thro' sunny morn the praises tell,
  Of sights and sounds in Galilee.

3 And when I read the thrilling lore
  Of him who walked upon the sea,
  I long, oh, how I long once more
  To follow him in Galilee.

34. The Master Calleth for Thee.

M. B. C. Slade. — Read John 11: 28, 29. — R. M. McIntosh, by per.

1. Her sad vigil keeping, Mary sat weeping, Mourning for Lazarus dead, Her glad tidings learning, Martha returning, Unto the weeping one said, Jesus is coming, him have I met, Glad are his tidings to me; Joyful arise, the Master is coming, Jesus is calling for thee.

2 Then swift at his calling, at his feet falling
  Mary so sorrowful goes;
  And trustful believing, meekly receiving,
  Hope that the Master bestows.

3 When loss is before us, grief gathers o'er us,
  Shadows of sorrow surround;
  Whate'er may befall us, if he will call us,
  Gladly we'll follow the sound.

35. Are There Ten Today?

Mrs. E. C. Ellsworth. — Read Luke 17: 12, 13. — Chas. Edw. Prior.

1. There were ten who stood as the Lord passed by, Calling for help with a thrilling cry; They were needy—sick; but with help at hand, Surely in silence they ne'er would stand. Are there

Are There Ten Today? Concluded.

2. There were ten believed in the joyful news,
Jesus, the Saviour, would ne'er refuse;
He was near at hand - they would call today,
Surely their cry would his footsteps stay.

3. There were ten partook of the healing power,
Asking, received from his hand that hour;
There were ten that day who to Jesus cried;
Surely, today there'll be none denied.

36 Jesus in Gethsemane.

H. S. H. SANDERS.

Copyright, 1892, by R. M. McIntosh.

1. See him in the garden lone,
Midnight darkness o'er him,
None but God to hear his moan;
Naught but death before him.

2. All his friends forsake him now;
None with him are staying;
Bloody sweat upon his brow,
To his Father praying.

3. On him all our sins were laid,
Thro' him came salvation;
He for us a ransom paid,
Priceless, pure oblation.

4. "Man of sorrows!" born to grief!
For our sins atoning,
By whose stripes we find relief,
Our lost state bemoaning.

37. He Was Despised.

W. A. O.
W. A. OGDEN.

By permission.

1 He was despised and rejected of men,
  The man of many sorrows was taken and slain;
  Cruel hands have nailed him upon the rugged tree,
  And thus he suffered even death for me.

CHORUS.—Now thanks be to God! thanks be to God!
  Who giveth us the victory through Jesus' blood;
  Over death he triumphed, and over all his foes,
  The world's Redeemer from the grave arose!

2 He was despised and rejected of men,
  But by his stripes we're healed from the wounding of sin;
  By his resurrection from death and from the grave,
  I am persuaded he alone can save.

3 He was despised and rejected of men,
  O sing the melting story again and again!
  Tell it to the nations that all the world may know,
  That from this fountain living waters flow.

On the Cross.

1 On the cross the Saviour hanging,
  Bled and died for you and me;
  Wondrous love! O! who can know it!
  Boundless, priceless, full and free!

CHORUS.—On the cross behold him hanging,
  On the blood-stain'd cross for me;
  Jesus died to bring salvation,
  Jesus died for you and me.

2 O, the blood-stain'd cross of Jesus,
  How it fills my soul with peace,
  As I there behold him dying,
  Bringing naught but my release.

3 'Tis indeed a truth most precious,
  That for sinners Jesus died,
  And we have a full remission
  Through a Savior crucified.

39. Story of the Cross.

Rev. W. P. Rivers. — R. M. McIntosh.

Oh, the gospel story tell, Of the cross! Let the echo rise and swell Of the cross!
of the cross! of the cross!

Sing the Savior's grief and woe, How his blood did free-ly flow, Till the children all shall know Of the cross!

D. S. blood did free-ly flow, Till the chil-dren all shall know Of the cross.

CHORUS.

Of the cross, . . . of the cross, ... Sing the Sav-ior's grief and woe, How his
Of the cross on which the bless-ed Savior died,

By permission.

2 Let us plead the holy name
    Of the cross!
  And the Saviour's pain and shame
    Of the cross!
  For his name must be our plea,
  For salvation full and free,
  And in death our hope must be
    Of the cross!

3 O, the song shall never cease
    Of the cross!
  Of the mercy, grace and peace,
    Of the cross!
  For its glory gilds the way,
  And it hath immortal ray,
  And we'll sing in heav'n for aye
    Of the cross!

40. Cross of Jesus.

Fred Woodrow. — Chas. H. Gabriel.

Cross of Jesus,—blessed symbol Of his sac-ri-fice and death; Voice of love, and mercy's message, Born of his expiring breath.

By permission.

Cross of Jesus. Concluded.

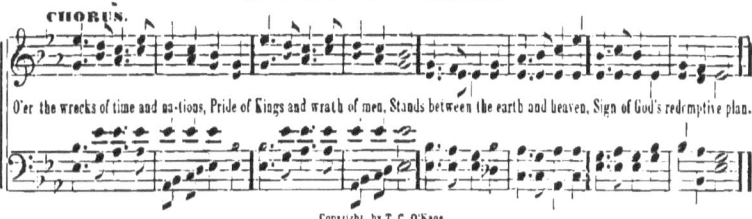

Copyright, by T. C. O'Kane.

1 Cross of Jesus,—blessed symbol
   Of his sacrifice and death ;
   Voice of love, and mercy's message,
   Born of his expiring breath.

2 Here the world may bring its sorrow,
   Here the world may leave its sin ;
   Tribes and nations seek a refuge,
   Find the door and enter in.

3 Prince and beggar, man and maiden,
   Find alike a common plea ;
   And the trumpets of salvation
   Sound a welcome far and free.

4 Here, O Christ, thy love adoring,
   I would thy salvation see ;
   And amid redemption's story,
   Wonder thou shouldst die for me.

41   Behold the Lamb.

Rev. C. W. Ray.   R. M. McIntosh.

Copyright, 1877, by R. M. McIntosh.

1 Behold the Lamb of Calvary—
   The bloody cross on which he dies ;
   He suffers there for you and me.
   O wondrous, wondrous sacrifice !

2 Behold the Lamb for sinners slain ;
   Betrayed, reviled and crucified ;
   The pierced hands, the gory stain,
   The nails, the spear and wounded side.

3 Behold the Lamb ! the rough thorn-crown
   Upon the dear Redeemer's brow ;
   While crimson streams are flowing down,
   Beneath his bleeding feet I bow.

4 Behold the Lamb ! who takes our sin and guilt away ;
   Beneath its precious cleansing flood
   My weary, trembling soul I lay.

42. Hallelujah! "He is Risen."

L. R. H. — W. S. MARTIN

1. Bless-ed morn of light and glo-ry, Bright'ning all the com-ing years; O-ver sin and death vic-to-rious, Christ, the ris-en Lord up-pears. Hal-le-lu-jah! "He is ris-en!" Sin and death bear sway no more; Je-sus reign-eth, Je-sus reign-eth O'er the earth for ev-er-more!

Copyright, 1885, by E. C. Avis.

2 Hail! all hail! our blessed Saviour,
Thou hast borne our griefs and woes
Thou hast pass'd the grave's dark portals,
Thou wilt conquer ev'ry foe.

3 Crown him! crown him! King and Saviour!
Let the earth give thanks and sing
Praises to our blest Redeemer,
Till the heav'ns with triumph ring.

43. Hallelujah! He is Risen.

ANON.

1 Christ, above all glory seated!
King eternal, strong to save!
To thee, Death, by death defeated,
Triumph high and glory gave.

2 Thou art gone where now is given
What no mortal might could gain,
On the eternal throne of heaven,
In thy Father's power to reign.

3 We, O Lord! with hearts adoring,
Follow thee above the sky:
Hear our prayers thy grace imploring,
Lift our souls to thee on high.

4 So when thou again in glory
On the clouds of heaven shall shine,
We, thy flock, shall stand before thee,
Owned for evermore as thine.

44. Christ Arose.

R. LOWRY. — R. LOWRY.

1. Low in the grave he lay—Je-sus, my Sav-iour; Wait-ing the com-ing day—Je-sus, my Lord. Up from the grave he a-

Christ Arose. Concluded.

2 Vainly they watch his bed —
   Jesus, my Saviour;
Vainly they seal the dead —
   Jesus, my Lord.

3 Death can not keep his prey —
   Jesus, my Saviour;
He tore the bars away —
   Jesus, my Lord.

45 He is Risen.

E. R. LATTA.   "He is not here, for he is risen as he said." — MATT. 28: 6.   A. J. ABBEY.

DUET. Joyous.

2 They are seeking for the Saviour,
   In the dampness and the gloom;
But he slumbers there no longer,
   They approach an empty tomb.

3 O, how sadly do they question,
   As in sorrow on they stray!

But behold the shining angel,
   He has rolled the stone away!

4 Weep no more, ye sad disciples,
   Your Redeemer ye shall see;
He is risen as he promised,
   Seek for him in Galilee.

Hallelujah! He Arose.

HARRIET E. JONES. "He is risen, as he said."—MATT. 28: 6. J. H. TENNEY, by per.

2 O'er all the earth the tidings spread,
  Ye Easter bells, ring loud and clear,
The Lord is risen from the dead,
  The Crucified again is here!

3 Yes, he arose, let men rejoice,
  Let holy angels shout and sing,
Let all the earth lift up its voice,
  The Christ arose to reign a King.

47. Ring the Bells.

1 Ring, ring the bells, the sweet gospel bells,
Echo their music o'er land and sea;
Jesus has risen the lost to save;
Ring to the world the victory.

2 Ring, ring the bells, the sweet gospel bells;
Jesus has risen to die no more;
Earth from her bondage of sin is free;
Ring out the news from shore to shore.

3 Ring, ring the bells, the sweet gospel bells;
Let hill and valley with praises ring;
Jesus has broken the bars of death;
Crown him, O crown him, Saviour, King.

48. Lift Up, O Little Children.

Mrs. T. F. Seward

2 Lift up, O tender lilies,
Your whiteness to the sun;
The earth is not our prison,
Since Christ himself hath risen,
The life of every one.

3 Ring, all ye bells, in welcome,
Your chimes of joy again!
Ring out the night of sadness,
Ring in the morn of gladness,
For death no more shall reign.

49. Jesus is Risen.

"But now is Christ risen from the dead."—1 Cor. 15: 20.

I. Baltzell, by per.

Jesus is Risen. Concluded.

2 Sad were the life we must part with tomorrow,
  If only death and the grave were our end;
  But Christ hath entered the valley of sorrow,
  Bids us arise, and to heaven ascend.

3 O, ye redeemed ones, proclaim the glad story,
  Lift your loud voices in triumph on high;
  Soon we shall sing with the angels in glory,
  Jesus is risen, and man shall not die.

50 Jesus Lives.

J. E. RANKIN.   "I am he that liveth and was dead."—REV. 1: 18.   E. S. LORENZ.

1. Jesus lives! lives a-gain! Hell's de-vic-es were in vain, Jesus lives, the cru-ci-fied! Tho' they nailed him to the tree, Brief their tri-umph was to be; All their mal-ice has he de-fied. Sound it a-broad that Je-sus lives! Sound it a-broad that Je-sus lives! Sound it a-broad that Je-sus lives! He lives for ev-er-more! more!

Used by permission of E. S. Lorenz, owner of the Copyright.

2 Jesus lives! lives and reigns!
  Sing in loud triumphal strains,
  Everywhere that death is found;
  How he rose for man who died,
  And death's gateway opened wide;
  Let the earth with the song resound.

3 Jesus lives, so shall I!
  Though this mortal waste and die,
  Though it molder in the grave;

Clothed in immortality,
  I shall yet my Jesus see,
  And in him life eternal have.

4 Jesus lives! perish earth!
  Perish all that time gives birth;
  Let the heavens together roll,
  Dire convulsions men appall,
  While they on the rocks do call:
  Jesus lives! thou art safe, my soul.

2. Out of the shadow of winter's long night,
   Earth comes in gladness today!
Clad in the garments of spring-time and light,
   Scattering doubt and dismay.
Beautiful story that never grows old,
   Pledge from our conquering Lord,
Earth is redeemed from its darkness and cold;
   Easter hath come at his word.

3. Out of the shadow of weakness and fear,
   Let us arise, then, today!
Jesus hath called us, our Easter is here!
   Why should we doubt and delay?
Here is the path that our Conqueror trod,
   Bright with his blessings of peace;
These are his blossoms that spring from the sod,
   Telling of hope and release.

52. The Lamb of Calvary.

J. H. MARTIN, D. D.   R. M. McINTOSH.

2 There is love, strong love, in the King on high
   To the souls condemned for their guilt,
   He will save the lost that to him draw nigh
   Thro' the precious blood that he spilt.

3 There is love, warm love, in the Saviour's heart
   For the troubled, wretched and weak;
   In his boundless grace he will peace impart
   To the mourner, lowly and meek.

4 Unto Jesus come with your load of grief,
   And repose by faith on his breast,
   There your burdened spirit shall find relief—
   On the Lamb of Calvary rest.

3 Once while resting on a pillow
   In the vessel, fast asleep,
There arose a mighty tempest
   On the wild and raging deep;
"Peace, be still," the Lord commanded,
   Every angry wave did stay ;
I am glad to tell you, children,
   He is just the same to-day.

4 Surely you have heard how Jesus
   Prayed down in Gethsemane,
How he shed his precious life-blood
   On the rugged, shameful tree.
Cruel thorns his forehead piercing,
   As his spirit passed away;
Children, won't you love and serve him?
   He is just the same to-day.

54 Once Again.

2 Once again the song ascending
  To the Lord who died for me;
Let me feel that he is hearing!
  How I long his face to see!
Mercy! mercy! like a fountain,
  Springing up and running o'er,
Life and love for thirsty millions,
  Life and love for millions more.

3 Once again, oh, tell the story
  Of the glory yet to be,
O'er the walls of shining jasper,
  O'er the bright and crystal sea;
I will listen, I will praise him,
  And amid a world of care,
Bear the cross without repining,
  Thinking of the glory there!

55. Cross of Jesus.

FRED. WOODROW. CHAS. H. GABRIEL.

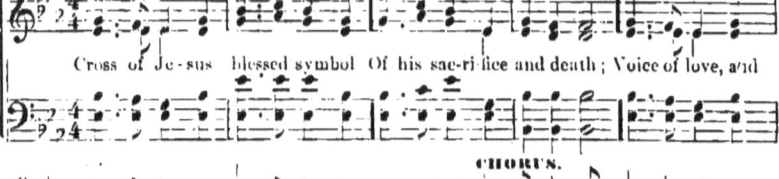

Cross of Je-sus blessed symbol Of his sac-ri-fice and death; Voice of love, and mercy's message, Born of his expiring breath. O'er the wrecks of time and na-tions, Pride of kings and wrath of man, Stands between the earth and heaven, Sign of God's redemptive plan.

Copyright, by T. C. O'Kane.

1 Cross of Jesus, blessed symbol
Of his sacrifice and death;
Voice of love and mercy's message,
Born of his expiring breath.

2 Here the world may bring its sorrow,
Here the world may leave its sin;
Tribes and nations seek a refuge,
Find the door and enter in.

3 Prince and beggar, man and maiden,
Find alike a common plea;
And the trumpets of salvation,
Sound a welcome far and free.

4 Here, O Christ, thy love adoring,
I would thy salvation see;
And amid redemption's story,
Wonder thou shouldst die for me.

56. Must Jesus Bear the Cross?

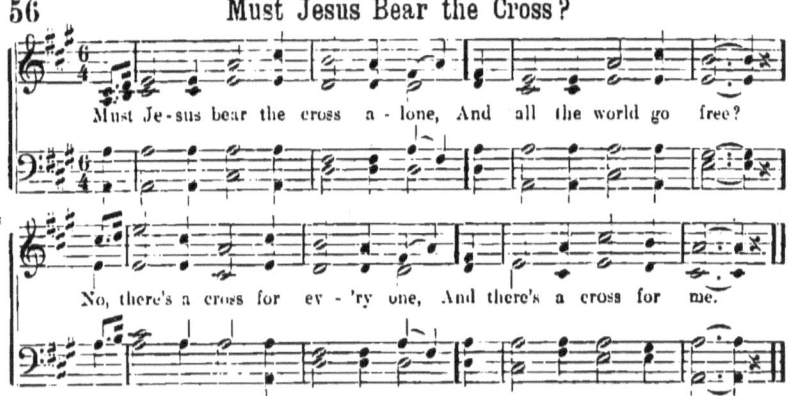

Must Je-sus bear the cross a-lone, And all the world go free? No, there's a cross for ev-'ry one, And there's a cross for me.

2 The consecrated cross I'll bear,
Till death shall set me free;
And then go home my crown to wear,
For there's a crown for me.

3 O precious cross! O glorious crown!
O resurrection day;
Ye angels, from the stars come down,
And bear my soul away.

57. Sinful Cities.

Mrs. M. B. C. Slade. — Read Matt. 10: 13–15. — R. M. McIntosh, by per.

1. Thou Bethsaida, the lovely, down beside the sea, Where the Master did his mighty works of love; By Genesareth he stands, And he stretches out his hands, And his voice resounds the waves above. O, Bethsaida, thy woe Floateth down the long ago; And its echo, sad and mournful, telleth me, If I follow not the word, The example of my Lord, Just so sad a sound for me may be.

2 Thou Capernaum, exalted, lifted up to heaven,
  If the mighty works that Jesus did in thee,
Tyre and Sidon once had seen,
They repentant both had been;
  In the judgment they more blest shall be.
O Capernaum, thy woe, etc.

3 O Bethsaida, Chorazin, fair Capernaum,
  Of your palaces no man can find a stone;
And Genesareth's blue wave
Softly sings beside your grave,
  And your glory from the earth is gone.
Sinful cities, now your woe, etc.

58. Unsearchable Riches.

F. J. CROSBY. J. R. SWENEY.

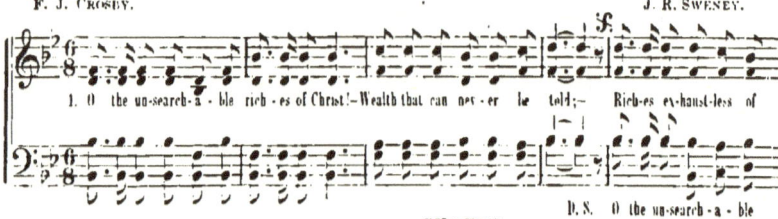

Used by permission of J. R. Sweney, owner of the Copyright.

1. O the unsearchable riches of Christ! –
Wealth that can never be told; –
Riches exhaustless of mercy and grace,
Precious, more precious than gold!

2. O the unsearchable riches of Christ,
Who shall their greatness declare;
Jewels whose luster our lives may adorn,
Pearls the poorest may wear.

3. O the unsearchable riches of Christ,
Freely, how freely they flow;
Making the souls of the faithful and true
Happy wherever they go.

4. O the unsearchable riches of Christ!
Who would not gladly endure
Trials, afflictions, and crosses on earth,
Riches like those to secure!

59. Ho, Every One That Thirsteth!

Isaiah 55: 1. FRANK M. DAVIS, by per.

LOVING AND PRAISING.

"I will praise Thee with my whole heart."—Ps. 138: 1.

65.   I will Sing with Joy.

J. H. MARTIN.   R. M. McINTOSH.

1. I will lift my voice in a song of praise, To my God and King I'll an anthem raise;
By the morning light, in the evening dim, I will sing with joy, I will worship him.

REFRAIN.
With the sun by day, and the stars by night, In a gladsome cho-rus at dawning light,
I will join with saints and with ser-a-phim, In a psalm of praise, in a joy-ful hymn.

Copyright, 1886, by R. M. McIntosh.

2 I will bless the Lord and extol his name,
I will laud his deeds and resound his fame;
I will sing his power on his throne above,
I will gladly tell of his grace and love.

3 In the house of God on the day of rest,
With a grateful heart, with a joyful breast,
I will sit and sing with the happy throng,
I will swell the notes of the choral song.

66. I Ought to Love my Saviour.

2 He left his home in glory,
To save my soul from death,
And now in all life's dangers,
He still sustains my breath.
I lay me down and slumber
All through the hours of night,
And wake again in safety
To hail the morning light.

3 It is but very little
For him that I can do;
Then let me seek to serve him,
My earthly journey through;
And without sigh or murmur,
To do his holy will;
And in my daily duties,
His wise commands fulfill.

4 And when I reach the mansion
He has prepared for me,
'Twill be my grateful pleasure
My Saviour's face to see.
And 'mid the angels' music,
Which then will greet my ear,
How eagerly I'll listen
My Saviour's voice to hear.

67. Praise to Jesus.

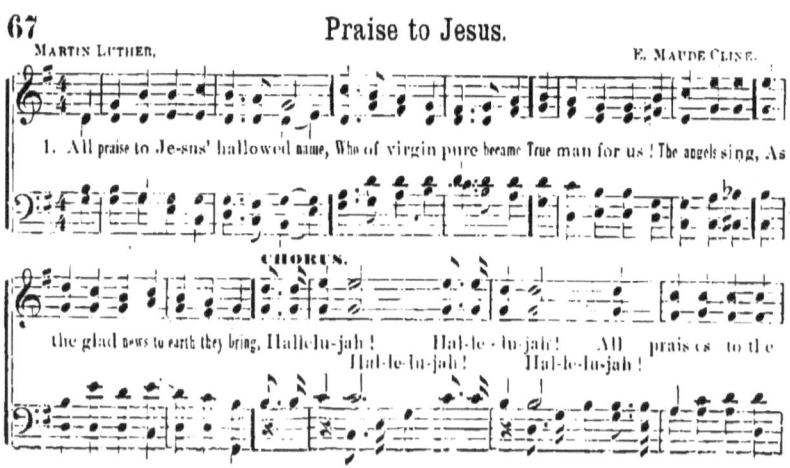

Praise to Jesus. Concluded.

2 The everlasting Father's Son
For a manger leaves his throne;
The mighty God, the eternal Good,
Hath clothed himself in flesh and blood.
  Hallelujah!

3 The eternal height, come down from heaven,
Hath to us new sunshine given;
It shineth in the midst of night
And maketh us the sons of light.
  Hallelujah!

4 The Father's Son, God ever blest,
In the world became a guest;
He leads us from this vale of tears
And makes us in his kingdom heirs.
  Hallelujah!

5 He came to earth so mean and poor,
Man to pity and restore,
And made us rich in heaven above,
Equal with angels through his love.
  Hallelujah!

6 All this he did to show his grace
To our poor and sinful race;
For this let Christendom adore
And praise his name for evermore.
  Hallelujah!

68 I Will Tell Jesus.

"Went and told it to Jesus."—MATT. 14: 12.

JULIA H. JOHNSTON.   LUCY J. RIDER. By per.

2 When I am joyous in the glad sunshine,
  I will tell him who loves me so,
Surely my Saviour waiteth to hear it,
  Every sweet secret he shall know.

3 When I'm in danger, when I'm in darkness,
  Tempted to think no helper near,
Still I'll run to him, tell him the story,
  Ask him to keep from harm and fear.

4 Trouble and sorrow drive me to Jesus,
  Whom beside him, on earth, have I?
Others may love me, Jesus can save me,
  Jesus will hear me when I cry.

5 If I am tempted, if I distrust him,
  If I forget and go astray,
Still I'll return and tell it to Jesus,
  Ask him to keep me every day.

69. Tell the Joyful Tidings.

J. W. McGarvey, Jr.   J. W. McGarvey, Jr.

Bless-ed be the name of Christ, our Sav-ior, Fill his courts with joyful praise, Un-to him the King and Lord of glo-ry, We our cheerful voices raise. Sing of him who left his home of glo-ry, On the cross to bleed and groan,

CHORUS.

Tell to all the world the wondrous sto-ry, Pointing them to his bright home. Tell the joyful tidings, friends of Je-sus,

Rit.

Oh, his wondrous love pro-claim, Come in-to his courts with thankful hearts, And praise the blessed Saviour's name.

Copyright 1892, by C. C. Cline.

1 Blessed be the name of Christ our Saviour,
Fill his courts with joyful praise;
Unto him, the King and Lord of Glory,
We our joyful voices raise.
Sing of him who left his home of glory,
On the cross to bleed and groan ;
Tell to all the world the wondrous story,
Pointing them to his bright home.

CHORUS.—Tell the joyful tidings, friends of Jesus,
Oh, his wondrous love proclaim,
Come into his courts with thankful hearts
And praise the blessed Saviour's name.

2 For the dear Redeemer's loving kindness
Grateful may we always be ;
We were all in bondage, sin, and blindness
Till he came and set us free.
Christians, hear him saying, "Tell the story,
'Work ye while 'tis called to-day,'
Work, and you shall rest in heavenly glory,
Toil and labor, watch and pray."—Cho.

3 Jesus is the friend of all who serve him,
Love him and obey his word ;
He will give to all a heavenly mansion,
"Enter in," will say the Lord.
Come, ye heavy laden, come to Jesus,
Hear his loving voice to-day ;
Cast on him your care and heavy burden,
Seek the realms of endless day.—Cho.

70. Tell Me All about Jesus.

ELISHA A. HOFFMAN.   CHAS. EDW. POLLOCK.

2 Tell me all about Jesus,
  The Lamb of Calvary;
  Tell me more of his mercy,
  More of his grace to me.

3 Tell me all about Jesus,
  Who daily cares for me;

Tell me why he should love me,
  Why he should die for me.

4 Tell me all about Jesus,
  Repeat the story o'er;
  Never shall I grow weary,
  Hearing it more and more.

71. Give Me Jesus.

"The love of Christ constraineth us."—2 Cor. 5:14.

FANNY J. CROSBY.   JOHN R. SWENEY.

By permission of J. R. Sweney, owner of the Copyright.

2 Take the world, but give me Jesus,
  Sweetest comfort of my soul;
  With my Saviour watching o'er me,
  I can sing though billows roll.

3 Take the world, but give me Jesus,
  Let me see his constant smile;

Then throughout my pilgrim journey,
  Light will cheer me all the while.

4 Take the world, but give me Jesus;
  In his cross my trust shall be,
  Till, with clearer, brighter vision,
  Face to face my Lord I see.

72. Revive Us Again.

WM. PATON MACKAY.   J. J. HUSBAND.

1. We praise thee, O God! for the Son of thy love, For Jesus who died, and is now gone above.

CHORUS.
Hallelujah! Thine the glory; Hallelujah! Amen!
Hallelujah! Thine the glory; (Omit.) . . . . . Revive us again.

2 We praise thee, O God! for thy Spirit of light,
Who has shown us our Saviour and scattered our night.
3 All glory and praise to the Lamb that was slain,
Who has borne all our sins, and has cleansed every stain.
4 All glory and praise to the God of all grace,
Who has bought us, and sought us, and guided our ways.
5 Revive us again; fill each heart with thy love;
May each soul be rekindled with fire from above.

73. Beautiful Songs.

FANNY J. CROSBY.   JNO. R. SWENEY.

Beautiful songs that here we sing, Lifting the heart to Jesus, Beautiful thought of joy they bring, Lifting the heart to Jesus.

REFRAIN.
Telling of home, of rest and love, Waiting for us in heav'n above; Beautiful songs, oh, beautiful songs, Lifting the heart to Jesus.

Copyright 1887, by John R. Sweney.

1 Beautiful songs that here we sing,
   Lifting the heart to Jesus,
Beautiful thoughts of joy they bring,
   Lifting the heart to Jesus.

2 Beautiful songs that cheer our way,
   Lifting the heart to Jesus,
Tenderly sweet from day to day,
   Lifting the heart to Jesus.

3 Beautiful songs of praise so dear,
   Lifting the heart to Jesus,
Drawing our faith to God more near,
   Lifting the heart to Jesus.

4 Beautiful songs that ne'er shall die,
   Lifting the heart to Jesus,
Floating in light from realms on high,
   Lifting the heart to Jesus.

74. Happy Greeting.

E. L. WHITE.

2 Our Father in Heaven, we lift up to thee,
Our voice of thanksgiving, our glad jubilee;
Oh, bless us and guide us, dear Saviour, we pray,
That from thy blessed precepts we never may stray.

3 And if, ere this glad year has drawn to a close,
Some loved one among us in death shall repose,
Grant, Lord, that the dear one in Heaven may dwell,
In the mansions of Jesus where all shall be well.

75. Morning Hymn.

T. O. SUMMERS. "Make me like unto thee." W. M. TRELOAR.

2 All through the day, I humbly pray,
  Be thou my guard and guide;
My sins forgive, and let me live,
  Dear Saviour, near thy side.

3 O, make me rest within thy breast,
  Dear Saviour of all grace;
Then I shall be, if made like thee,
  Prepared to see thy face.

76. No One Like Jesus.

"Greater love hath no man than this, that a man lay down his life for his friends."—JOHN xv: 13.

ANNA SHARF. S. M. LUTZ.

by permission.

2 Tho' we so often thoughtlessly stray
Out of the straight path and out of the way,
Ever he follows out in the night,
Kindly he guides us back to the light.

3 Who is like Jesus, tender and true?
Whose love like Jesus' love for me and you?
Ever we'll praise him, ever we'll sing,
Jesus our Saviour, Master, and King!

77. Praise Him.

E. ALBRIGHT.

Copyright, 1881, by O. Ditson & Co.

78. Praise! Give Praise.

FANNY CROSBY.   CHESTER G. ALLEN.

1. Praise him, praise him—Jesus, our blessed Redeemer, Sing, O earth, his wonderful love proclaim.
Hail him! hail him! highest archangels in glory, Strength and honor give to his holy name.
D.S. O ye saints that dwell on the mountain of Zion, Praise him, praise him ever in joyful song.

Like a shepherd Jesus will guard his children, In his arms he carries them all day long.

Copyright, 1869, by Biglow & Main. Used by permission.

2 Praise him, praise him—Jesus our blessed Redeemer,
  For our sins he suffered and bled and died;
He, our rock, our hope of eternal salvation,
  Hail him, hail him, Jesus, the Crucified.
Loving Saviour, meekly enduring sorrow,
  Crowned with thorns that cruelly pierced his brow;
Once for us rejected, despised, and forsaken,
  Prince of Glory, he is triumphant now.

3 Praise him, praise him, Jesus, our blessed Redeemer,
  Heavenly portals, loud with hosannas ring,
Jesus, Saviour, reigneth for ever and ever;
  Crown him, crown him—Prophet and Priest and King.
Death is vanquished! Tell it with joy, ye faithful.
  Where is now thy victory, boasting grave?
Jesus lives! No longer thy portals are cheerless;
  Jesus lives, the mighty and strong to save.

Praise Him. Concluded.

2 All the earth is bright and glad,
  Cheerily, cheerily sing!
Why should we be ever sad?
  Let us praise our King.

3 Jesus loves us tenderly,
  Happily, happily sing!

Says—Oh! bring them unto me,
  All the children bring.

4 Let each heart rejoice to-day,
  Joyfully, joyfully sing!
Oh! be happy while you may,
  Praise your Lord and King.

79. Valens.

1. Glo-ry and praise and hon-or To thee, Redeem-er, King, To whom the lips of chil-dren Made sweet ho-san-nas ring. Glo-ry and praise and hon-or, To thee, Redeem-er, King, To whom the lips of chil-dren Made sweet ho-san-nas ring.

2 The people of the Hebrews
With palms before thee went;
Our praise and prayer and anthems
Before thee we present.

3 Thou wentest to thy passion
Amid their shouts of praise;

Thou reignest now in glory,
While we our anthems raise.

4 Thou didst accept their praises;
Accept the prayers we bring,
Who in all good delightest,
Thou good and gracious King!

80. He Loved You and Me.

Miss P. J. Owens.   "Behold how he loved him."—John 11: 36.   Harry Sanders.

1. In the Sun-day-school ar-my our names are enrolled, And we fol-low our Lead-er, all stead-fast and bold; On the Sun-day-school ban-ner his name you may see; It is Je-sus, our Sav-ior, who loved you and me.

He Loved You and Me. Concluded.

2 We are young, but his wisdom shall guide us aright;
We are weak, but his strength is our courage and might;
When we follow his standard the darkness will flee,
And our watchword is always, "He loved you and me."

3 In our childhood we come, if no ripe sheaves be ours,
We will garland his pathway with blossoms and flowers;
We will go forth at morning, his gleaners to be,
He will welcome us smiling, who loves you and me.

4 When the victory is won, and the conflict is o'er,
We will close, round our leader, on Canaan's bright shore;
Then we'll sing on, exulting his glory to see,
For we'll dwell with him ever, who loves you and me.

81   The Precious Love of Jesus.

FANNY J. CROSBY.   W. J. KIRKPATRICK.

2 'Tis love that conquers every fear,
    The precious love of Jesus,
And now by faith has brought us near
    The bleeding side of Jesus.

3 'Tis love that fills the joyful heart,
    And draws it up to Jesus,
Where neither life nor death can part
    The sacred bonds from Jesus.

4 When faith and hope have ceas'd to shine,
    And we are safe with Jesus,
We'll praise the power of love divine
    That brought us home to Jesus.

82. Come with Cheerful Singing.

"Enter into his gates with thanksgiving."—Ps. 100: 4.

MISS M. P. A. CROZIER.   W. A. OGDEN.

1. Come with cheerful sing-ing, Serve the Lord with gladness, Come with lov-ing spir-it to his courts to-day,
Lift the heart to Je-sus, Thank him for the sun-shine, Thank him for the sweetness of his grace al-way.

REFRAIN.

Thank him for his grace, Thank him for his grace, Thank him for the sweetness of his grace al-way.
Mu-sic of his voice,
To the place of prayer,

O thank him,   O thank him,

Copyright, 1885, by W. A. Ogden.

2 "Let the little children," hear the Saviour saying,
   "Let the little loving children come to me."
He, the gentle Shepherd, takes them on his bosom,
Oh, how sweet the music of his voice must be.

3 Out into the highways, out into the hedges,
   Go and find the children idly playing there.
Many lambs are straying far away from Jesus,
Go and bring them hither to the house of prayer.

83. A Friend that's Ever Near.

"Fear not, for I am with thee."   W. B. BRADBURY.

Quick.

1. { Tho' the days are dark with troub-le, And thy heart is filled with fear, There is one that sees thee ev-er,
    Cheer-ful hearts and smil-ing fac-es Oft-en make thee hap-py here, Yet no one was e'er so hap-py,

REFRAIN.

And will hold thee near and dear, }
But sometimes the clouds ap-pear. } There's a friend that's ev-er near, Nev-er fear, He is ev-er near.

Used by permission of The Biglow & Main Co., owners of the Copyright.

A Friend that's Ever Near. Concluded.

Nev-er, nev-er fear, There's a friend that's ev-er near, Nev-er fear, he is ev-er near, Nev-er fear.

2 All thy prospects will seem brighter
  When the shadow leaves the heart,
  And the steps of time beat lighter
  When the gloomy clouds depart.
  Many days have dawned serenely,
  While the birds sang with delight,
  But the skies were dark and gloomy
  Ere the sun had reached its height.

3 Soon will dawn a brighter morning
  On a blessèd, tranquil shore;
  Sighs will then give place to singing,
  Tears to bliss, for evermore.
  Thou shalt see a world of glory,
  And eternal joy and bliss;
  Let not, then, thy soul be moaning
  O'er the woes and cares of this.

84 Worthy is the Lamb.

C. H. G. CHAS. H. GABRIEL.

1. Hark! the voice of countless thousands singing, "Worthy is the Lamb that was slain!" All the mighty hosts of heaven joining: "Worthy is the Lamb that was slain!" Hear the heav'nly chorus ringing,

CHORUS.

'Round the throne for-ev-er sing-ing, Worth-y is the Lamb, worth-y is the Lamb, Worth-y is the Lamb that was slain.

Used by permission of Chas. H. Gabriel, owner of the Copyright.

2 Who will join to chant the wondrous story,
  "Worthy is the Lamb that was slain!"
  Who will join the choirs of highest glory:
  "Worthy is the Lamb that was slain!"

3 Let each heart be fill'd with emulation!
  "Worthy is the Lamb that was slain!"
  Let them chant the notes of full salvation!
  "Worthy is the Lamb that was slain!"

4 Life or death eternal, everlasting:
  "Worthy is the Lamb that was slain!"
  Honor, glory, riches, pow'r, and blessing!
  "Worthy is the Lamb that was slain!"

85. Welcome, Jesus, Welcome.

REV. J. B. ATCHINSON. FRANK L. ARMSTRONG.

1. In the ark most holy, Once the Lord appear'd, There to bless his people, Who his mandate fear'd; Wheresoe'er this symbol Found a resting place, There were sweetest tokens, Of Jehovah's grace.

CHORUS.
Welcome, Jesus, welcome, Welcome in my heart, Make it now thy dwelling-place, And nev-er more depart, Make it now thy dwelling-place, And nev-er more de-part.

By permission.

2 Now God's chosen temple,
Where he will impart
Heaven's richest blessings,
Is my sinful heart;
At the door he's knocking,
Waiting to come in,—
Welcome, Jesus, welcome,
Cleanse my heart from sin.

3 Wheresoever Jesus
Is a welcome guest,
In the heart or household,
There is sweetest rest;
Welcome, blessed Saviour,
Show me now thy grace,
Make my heart thy temple,
Thine own dwelling-place.

86. Jesus is King.

ROBERT MORRIS, LL. D. W. A. OGDEN.

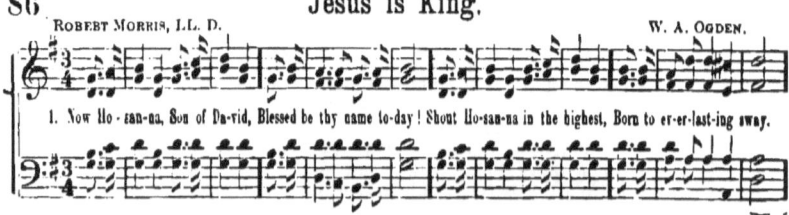

1. Now Ho-san-na, Son of Da-vid, Blessed be thy name to-day! Shout Ho-san-na in the highest, Born to ev-er-last-ing sway.

Jesus is King. Concluded.

2 Blessed be the king of Judah,
  Peace and glory in the sky!
  In the name of God he cometh,
  Here to rule eternally.
  Mighty doors, your bolts unbrace,
  Let the Lord of glory pass;
  Shout Hosanna, shout and sing,
  Jesus Christ, the Lord, is King.

3 Glory to the Conq'ring Hero,
  Not with strength of warrior swords,
  His the might of earth and heaven,
  King of kings, and Lord of lords.
  Hearts of stone, oh, melt and move,
  Open to the Lord of love;
  Shout Hosanna, shout and sing,
  Jesus Christ, the Lord, is King.

87 A Blessing in Prayer.

E. E. HEWITT. WM. J. KIRKPATRICK.

Copyright, 1887, by Wm. J. Kirkpatrick.

2 There is grace to help in our time of need,
  For our friend above is a friend indeed,
  We may cast on him every grief and care;
  There is always a blessing, a blessing in prayer.

3 When our songs are glad with the joy of life,
  When our hearts are sad with its ills and strife,
  When the powers of sin would the soul ensnare,
  There is always a blessing, a blessing in prayer.

4 There is perfect peace, though the wild waves roll;
  There are gifts of love for the seeking soul,
  Till we praise the Lord in his home so fair,
  There is always a blessing, a blessing in prayer.

88. Children's Te Deum.

MRS. LOULA KENDALL ROGERS. EMILIUS LAROCHE.

1. Let us meet at early dawn At the mercy seat, When sweet birds and flowers fair Songs of praise repeat.
In the freshness of our youth, Ere the sun's bright rays Pass away amid the cloud, Let us sing God's praise.

REFRAIN.
Let us sing his praise, Let us sing his praise, In the morn-ing and the even-ing, Let us sing his praise.
As we journey on our way, Let us sing his praise, Draw-ing near-er day by day, Let us sing his praise.

Copyright, 1880, by R. L. McIntosh.

2 Let us haste to hear his word
Ere the day be past,
For the night with fearful storm
May the sky o'ercast.
How we love to sing his praise
When the heart is young,
Never sweeter song than this
Hath a nation sung!

3 Let the pleasures of the world
Fail our hearts to win,
For we'll battle ev'ry day
'Gainst the pow'r of sin.
Oh, how sweet to consecrate
All our youthful days
To the service of the Lord,
As we sing his praise!

89. I'll Sing the Praise of Jesus.

FRANK M. DAVIS. FRANK M. DAVIS.

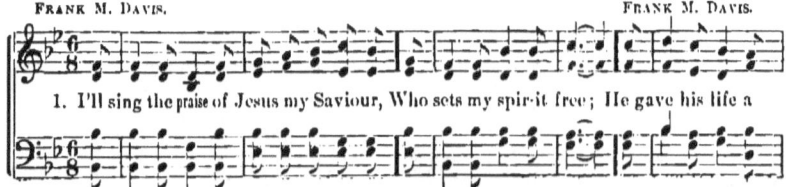

1. I'll sing the praise of Jesus my Saviour, Who sets my spir-it free; He gave his life a

I'll Sing the Praise of Jesus. Concluded.

2 I'll sing the praise of Jesus my Saviour,
  And tell his love abroad;
  He fills my soul with rapture, rejoicing,
  He leads me home to God.

3 I'll sing the praise of Jesus my Saviour,
  Who hears my feeblest cry;
  A Friend in times of sorrow and trouble,
  A Friend that's ever nigh.

90 I Will Praise the Lord To-day.

"With my song will I praise him."—Ps. 28: 7.

E. A. BARNES. WM. J. KIRKPATRICK.

2 I will praise the Lord to-day,
  For his name is more than sweet:
  And I gather strength for the toils of life
  As I worship at his feet.

3 I will praise the Lord to-day,
  For his word is life and love;

And the hope he gives is a blessed hope,
  For it lifts my soul above.

4 I will praise the Lord to-day,
  For the Lord has ransomed me;
  He has set his seal on this soul of mine,
  That his glory I may see.

91. I Will Sing for Jesus.

PHILIP PHILLIPS.

1. I will sing for Jesus, With his blood he bought me; And all along my pilgrim way His loving hand has brought me.

CHORUS.
O, help me sing for Jesus, Help me tell the story Of him who did redeem us, The Lord of life and glory.

By permission.

2 Can there overtake me
  Any dark disaster,
  While I sing for Jesus,
  My blessed, blessed Master?

3 I will sing for Jesus!
  His name alone prevailing,
  Shall be my sweetest music,
  When heart and flesh are failing.

4 Still I'll sing for Jesus!
  O, how will I adore him,
  Among the cloud of witnesses,
  Who cast their crowns before him.

92. Singing for Jesus.

Moderato. PHILIP PHILLIPS.

1. Singing for Jesus, singing for Jesus, Trying to serve him wherever I go; Pointing the lost to the way of salvation—This be my mission, a pilgrim below. When in the

By permission.

Singing for Jesus. Concluded.

2 Singing for Jesus glad hymns of devotion,
　Lifting the soul on her pinions of love;
　Dropping a word or a thought by the wayside,
　Telling of rest in the mansions above.
　Music may soften where language would fail us,
　Feelings long buried 't will often restore;
　Tones that were breathed from the lips of departed,
　How we revere them when they are no more.

3 Singing for Jesus, my blessed Redeemer,
　God of the pilgrims, for thee I will sing;
　When o'er the billows of time I am wafted,
　Still with thy praise shall eternity ring.
　Glory to God for the prospect before me,
　Soon shall my spirit transported ascend;
　Singing for Jesus, O blissful employment,
　Loud hallelujahs that never will end.

93　Everlasting Praise.

C. H. G.　　　　　　　　　　　　　　　　　　CHAS. H. GABRIEL.

2 Praise the Lord in song and in secret pray'r,
　Young and aged bow before him;
Coming in the name of the crucified,
　In humility adore him.

3 Praise the Lord in song, hallelujahs sing,
　Glorify his name forever;
For he bore the sins of a fallen world,
　And he will forsake us never.

94. Singing From the Heart.

"I will sing with the spirit, and I will sing with the understanding also."—1 Cor. 14: 15.

ROBT. MORRIS, LL. D. H. R. PALMER, by per.

1. If you have a pleas-ant tho't, Sing it, sing it, Like the bird-ies in their sport, Sing it from the heart;
Does the Ho-ly Spir-it move For the tam'kins of his love, Sing and point the fold a-bove, Sing it from the heart.

CHORUS.

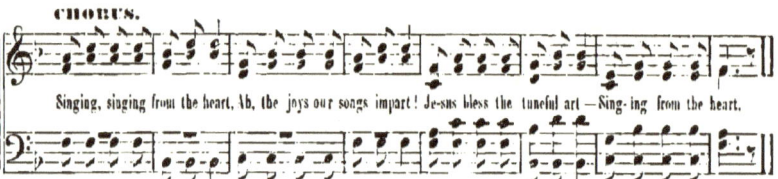

Singing, singing from the heart, Ah, the joys our songs impart! Je-sus bless the tuneful art—Sing-ing from the heart.

2 Every gracious love of his,
Sing it, sing it;
Nothing sounds so well as this—
Sing it from the heart;
How he walked upon the wave,
Rescued Lazarus from the grave,
Died, our guilty souls to save,
Sing it from the heart.

3 Are you weary? are you sad?
Sing it, sing it;
Make yourselves and others glad—
Sing it from the heart;
Angels up before his face
Sing of his redeeming grace;
Give the Saviour endless praise,
Sing it from the heart.

95. Worship in Spirit.

"Exalt ye the Lord our God, and worship at his footstool."

DR. THOMAS HASTINGS.

With emphasis.

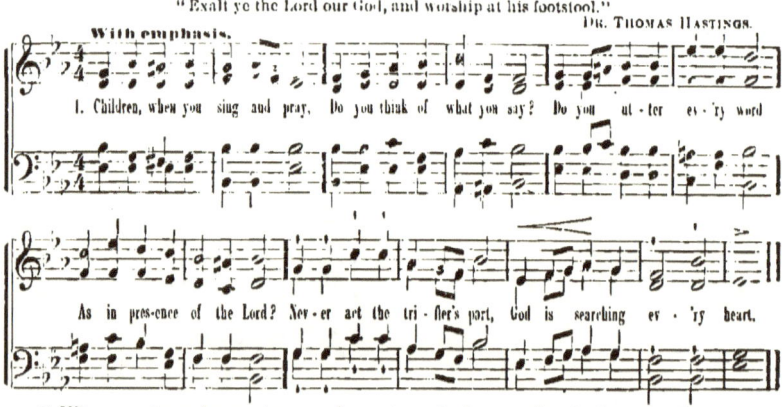

1. Children, when you sing and pray, Do you think of what you say? Do you ut-ter ev-'ry word As in pres-ence of the Lord? Nev-er act the tri-fler's part, God is searching ev-'ry heart.

2 When you hear the precious word,
Giv'n to us by Christ the Lord,
Do you keep it still in mind?
Are your thoughts to him inclined?
Never act the trifler's part,
God is searching every heart.

3 Are you ready to believe
The instructions you receive?
When you think of what you hear,
Is the meaning dark or clear?
Never act the trifler's part,
God is searching every heart.

4 When you leave the house of God,
Happy in the homeward road,
Keeping still the holy day,
Do not loiter by the way;
Never act the trifler's part,
God is searching every heart.

96. Worthy is the Lamb.

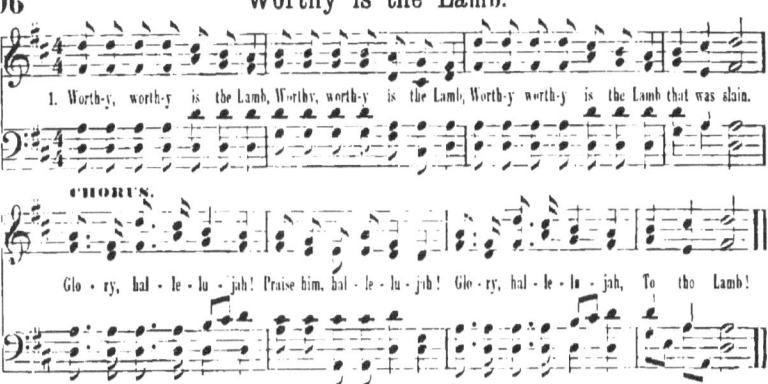

2 Sons of morning, sing his praise,
In the noblest strains you raise,
Man's redemption claims your lays,
  Praise the Lamb.

3 Christ has come in very deed,
Born to bruise the serpent's head;
Sinner, he's the friend you need,
  Praise the Lamb.

4 See, in sad Gethsemane,
See, on tragic Calvary,
Sinner, see his love to thee,
  Praise the Lamb.

5 Thus may we each moment feel,
Love him, serve him, praise him still,
Till we all on Zion's hill
  See the Lamb.

97. The Royal Proclamation.

W. B. BRADBURY.

Used by permission of The Biglow & Main Co., owners of the Copyright.

2 See the royal banner flying,
Hear the heralds loudly crying,
"Rebel sinners, royal favor
Now is offered by the Saviour."

3 "Here is wine, and milk, and honey;
Come, and purchase without money;
Mercy flowing from a fountain,
Streaming from the holy mountain."

4 Shout, ye tongues of every nation,
To the bounds of the creation;
Shout the praise of Judah's Lion,
The Almighty Prince of Zion.

5 Shout, ye saints, make joyful mention,
Christ hath purchased our redemption;
Angels, shout the pleasing story,
Through the brighter worlds of glory.

100. I will Trust in my Saviour.

"I will lead them in paths they have not known."—Isaiah 41:16.

MRS. LOULA K. ROGERS. R. M. McINTOSH, by per.

1 Tho' the shadows gather o'er my pathway here,
   And no sun comes with joyous ray,
   In the darkness not an evil will I fear,
   For my Saviour is leading the way.

REFRAIN.—I will trust in my Saviour, I will trust in my Saviour,
   I will trust in my Saviour alway;
   He will lead me thro' the night, by his ever shining light,
   I will trust in my Saviour to-day!

2 In the tempest, when the winds around me roll,
   And the thunders my heart affright,
   Sweetly comes a loving whisper to my soul,
   Then the world is all beauty and light.

3 When the chilling blight of death is on my brow,
   And the earth passes from my view,
   Simply trusting in my Saviour then, as now,
   He will lead me in paths ever new.

Sweet it is to Know.

Words and music by C. R. REED.

1 Sweet it is to know that Jesus loves us still,
If we but obey and do his holy will,
He will safely guide us to that happy land,
Where we'll dwell forever, with the angel band.

2 Now the Saviour calls us, hear his voice to-day,
Listen to his teaching, listen and obey.
Life for you and me has Jesus promised free,
Come to him, dear children, ever happy be.

3 Jesus died to save us, now he reigns above,
Ever interceding with unbounded love.
Boldly then press forward, ever faithful be,
Seek a home in heaven, life eternally.

WORKING FOR JESUS.

[Especially adapted to Y. P. S. C. E. meetings.]

"*I must work the works of him that sent me while it is day: the night cometh when no man can work.*"—*John 9 : 4.*

105 The Whole Wide World.

J. DEXTER HAMMOND.   WM. J. KIRKPATRICK.

1. The whole wide world for Jesus, This shall our watchword be, Upon the highest mountain, Down by the widest sea, The whole wide world for Jesus, To him all men shall bow, In city or on prairie, The world for Jesus now.

CHORUS.
The whole wide world, the whole wide world, Proclaim the gospel tidings thro' the whole wide world, Lift up the cross for Jesus, His banner be unfurled, Till ev'ry tongue confess him, thro' the whole wide world.

Copyright, 1885, by John J. Hood

2 The whole wide world for Jesus,
  Inspires us with the thought
That ev'ry son of Adam
  Hath by the blood been bought.
The whole wide world for Jesus,
  Oh, faint not by the way!
The cross shall surely conquer,
  In this our glorious day.

3 The whole wide world for Jesus,
  The marching order sound,
Go ye and preach the gospel
  Wherever man is found.

The whole wide world for Jesus,
  Our banner is unfurled,
We battle now for Jesus,
  And faith demands the world.

4 The whole wide world for Jesus,
  In the Father's home above
Are many wondrous mansions,
  Mansions of light and love.
The whole wide world for Jesus,
  Ride forth, O conquering King,
Through all the mighty nations,
  The world to glory bring.

106. The Endeavor Band.

L. E. LINDSEY. JNO. R. SWENEY.

1 A Christian band from far and near,
  We meet to learn of Jesus here,
  To read his word whose every line
  Is full of hope and joy divine.

2 A Christian band where all may sing,
  Glad songs of praise to God our King,
  And youthful hearts may find the way
  To perfect peace and endless day.

3 Each willing hand and thankful heart
  Is bound again before we part,
  As sheaves on earth are bound with twine,
  His words shall bind as cords divine.

4 The Master's work we'll still pursue,
  And once again our pledge renew,
  To him who saves us by his love,
  Till gathered home with him above.

107. Welcome.

1. We welcome you, friends, to our meeting to-night,
   Where young people gather, the place of delight;
   To speak words of kindness, to sing and to pray,
   To help some poor wanderer to Jesus to-day.

   REFRAIN.—We welcome you here, from far and from near,
   Oh, may the blest Spirit each heart fill with cheer;
   May love peace and joy, now banish all fear,
   We welcome, we welcome, we welcome you here.

2. How blessed, how cheering, for all to unite
   Against satan's kingdom for God and the right;
   We pray that the Trinity, holy and true,
   May send a rich blessing just now opon to you.

3. We thank thee, O Father, for this blessed hour,
   Smile graciously on us, and grant us thy pow'r;
   Thy fullness of blessing on us now bestow,
   And make us thine own as we from this place go.

4. The tie that has long round us each been entwined,
   More closely, dear Saviour, our hearts with it bind,
   And help us our actions to center above,
   Until we, shall like thee, be perfect in love.

108. Come and Hear the Story Told.

"Hearken unto me, my people, and give ear unto me."—Is. 51: 4.

E. R. LATTA.   E. S. LORENZ.

Copyright, 1884, by E. S. Lorenz.

2 Oh, the poverty and woe
   That the Saviour took instead
Of the glory and riches
   That were all around him spread;
Yes, my eyes are mov'd to tears,
   And my heart to sympathy,
When I listen to the story
   Of the Saviour's love for me.

3 Just as sweet the story sounds
   Of the blessed Saviour's birth,
As it did to watching Shepherds
   When it first was born to earth;
Just as sweet the story seems,
   Tho' I've heard it o'er and o'er,
Of the Saviour's love and pity,
   Such as ne'er was shown before.

109 Do Something To-Day.

LANTA WILSON SMITH. WM. J. KIRKPATRICK.

Copyright, 1888, by Wm. J. Kirkpatrick.

2 Go rescue that wandering brother
  Who sinks 'neath his burden of woe,
A single kind action may save him,
  If love and compassion you show;
Don't shrink from the vilest about you,
  If you can but lead them from sin;
For this is the grandest of missons,—
  Lost souls for the Master to win.—CHO.

3 Go sing happy songs of rejoicing
  With those who no sorrows have known;
Go weep with the heart-broken mourner,
  Go comfort the sad and the lone;

From pitfalls and snares of the tempter
  Go rescue the thoughtless and wild:
Go win from pale lips a "God bless you,"
  Go brighten the life of a child.—CHO.

4 Oh, never, my brother, stand waiting,
  Be willing to do what you can;
The humblest service is needed,
  To fill out the Father's great plan;
Be earning your stars of rejoicing
  While earth-life is passing away;
Win some one to meet you in glory,—
  Do something for Jesus to-day.—CHO.

110. I Want to be a Worker.

"The laborers are few."—MATT. 9: 37.

I. B. / I. BALTZELL, by per.

1. I want to be a worker for the Lord; I want to love and trust his holy word; I want to sing and pray, and be

CHORUS.

toiling ev-ry day In the vineyard of the Lord. I will work, I will pray, In the vineyard, in the
and pray, and pray,
vineyard of the Lord. I will work, I will pray, I will la-bor ev - ry day In the vineyard of the Lord.
of the Lord;

2 I want to be a worker every day;
I want to lead the erring in the way
That leads to heaven above,
Where all is peace and love,
In the kingdom of the Lord.

3 I want to be a worker strong and brave;
I want to trust in Jesus' power to save;
All who will truly come,
Shall find a happy home
In the kingdom of the Lord.

111. Working for Jesus.

"Go ye also into the vineyard, and whatsoever is right, I will give you."—MATT. 20: 4.

J. H. MARTIN. / R. M. McINTOSH, by per.

1. Hear the voice of Je-sus say, Loud-ly cry-ing un-to all, In my vine-yard work to-day, Hearken to his call.

REFRAIN.

Work, then, for Je-sus. He will own and bless your la-bors; Work, work for Je-sus, Work, work to-day.

2 Why, he asks, through all the day,
Stand ye idle, nothing do?
Enter in without delay,
I have work for you.

3 Work and serve me with delight,
Full reward to you I'll give;
At the gathering shades of night,
Wages you'll receive.

112. What Can I Do for Jesus.

M. B. P.   E. MAUDE CLINE.

1. What can I do for Je-sus, Who's done so much for me? How can I tru-ly serve him now, Whose grace has set me free? So fee-ble and so sin-ful, So apt to go a-stray; What can I do but fol-low him, His meek and low-ly way!

Copyright, 1892, by C. C. Cline.

2 'Tis thus I'll serve my Saviour
By walking in his ways,—
And now I will devote to him
The remnant of my days;
With all my heart I'll love him,
And read his blessed Word,
And follow him in faith and truth,
And thus I'll serve the Lord.

3 Whatever Christ doth bid me,
That gladly will I do;
And where his guiding hand doth lead,
I cheerfully will go;
And this I'll do for Jesus –
I can do nothing more –
Oh, will he thus accept me when
I reach the heav'nly shore?

113. Harvest Time. 8s & 7s.

"The laborer is worthy of his hire."

DR. THOMAS HASTINGS.   C. S. CABLE.

1. He that goeth forth with weeping, Bearing precious seed of love, Nev-er tiring, nev-er sleeping, Findeth mercy from above.

CHORUS.

Lo! the scene of verdure bright'ning, In the rising grain ap-pear; See, the waving fields are whitening, For the harvest-time is near.
Lo! the scene of verdure bright'ning, In the rising grain appear; See, the waving fields are whitening.

2 Soft descend the dews of heaven,
Bright the rays celestial shine;
Precious fruits will thus be given,
Thro' the influence all divine.

3 Sow thy seed, be never weary,
Let no fears thy soul annoy;
Be the prospect ne'er so dreary,
Thou shalt reap the fruits of joy.

114. There's Much We Can Do.

"Whatsoever thy hand findeth to do, do it with thy might."—Eccl. 9: 10

Mrs. E. C. Ellsworth.   E. O. Excell.

1. There's much we can do if we work with a will, No time to be wasted to-day;
The Master is read-y our labors to bless, And (Omit) .... wages he offers to pay.

CHORUS.
No time to be wasted, for many the fields, And lab'rers, as ev-er, are few; .... A-way to the work that is need-ing a hand; So much! O so much we can do!

Copyright, 1885, by E. O. Excell.

2. So much we can do in the sowing of seed,
Some fields are yet barren and waste,
The foe will be busy in spreading the tares,
Then go, and be working with haste.

3. So much we can do in the reaping of wheat,
Some fields for the harvest are white;
So much may be lost when the harvest is past,
If left to the mildew and blight.

115. Let Us Work.

"I must work the works of him that sent me, while it is day."—John 9: 4.

J. B. Carlin.   I. Baltzell, by per.

1. Let us work, let us work in the vineyard to-day, Waiting not till the morrow's begun;

Let Us Work. Concluded

For the day of sal-va-tion is pass-ing a-way, And the dark gloomy night hastens on.
D. S. For the Master has promised a boun-ti-ful yield, When we meet on the heaven-ly plain.

CHORUS.

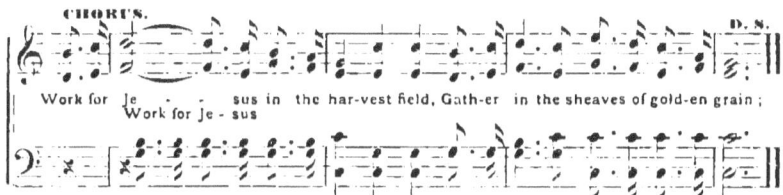

Work for Je - - sus in the har-vest field, Gath-er in the sheaves of gold-en grain;
Work for Je - sus

2 Let us work, let us work in the vineyard to-day,
Let us seek all the guilty to save;
Many souls may be lost if our work we delay,
And go down in despair to the grave.

3 Let us work, let us work in the vineyard to-day,
There is something for each one to do;
And the Master, at evening, your wages will pay,
Falter not, for they soon will be due.

116   The Battle Hymn of Missions.

RAY PALMER.   JOHN WHITAKER.

1. E - ter - nal Father, thou hast said, That Christ all glo - ry shall ob - tain;
That he who once a suff - 'rer bled Shall o'er the world a con-qu'ror reign.

2 We wait thy triumph, Saviour King;
Long ages have prepared thy way;
Now all abroad thy banner fling,
Set time's great battle in array.

3 Thy hosts are mustered to the field;
"The Cross! the Cross!" the battle call,
The old grim tow'rs of darkness yield
And soon shall totter to their fall.

4 On mountain tops the watchfires glow,
Where scatter'd wide the watchmen stand,
Voice echoes voice, and onward flow
The joyous shouts from land to land.

5 Oh, fill the Church with faith and pow'r,
Bid her long night of weeping cease;
To groaning nations haste the hour
Of life and freedom, light and peace.

117. This Lost World for Jesus.

J. E. RANKIN, D. D. — CHAS H. GABRIEL.

1. This lost, lost world for Je-sus! 'Twas heav'n he put a-side; On earth he walked in-car-nate, Was scourged and crucified, Then let the King Im-man-uel, Who left for us a throne, Re-turn and take pos-ses-sion, Return and claim his own.

CHORUS.
This lost, lost world for Jesus, This world, (lost world) for Jesus; This lost, lost world for Jesus, This world, (lost world) for Jesus.

Copyright, 1891, by Chas. H. Gabriel.

2 This lost, lost world for Jesus!
From where the rising sun
Lights up the orient mountains
To where his course is run;
He is the world's Redeemer,
Let all beneath the skies
Speak back to him, one language,
In hymns of praise arise.

3 This lost, lost world for Jesus!
The word that gave it birth
Can bring the dawn prophetic,
Can bring new heav'n and earth;
When main-land, sea and river,
When island, hill and plain
Shall catch the glow of Eden,
Smile back to heav'n again.

4 This lost, lost world for Jesus.
He comes to make it bloom;
Be ready for the signal,
Prepare his kingdom room;
Until he comes to take us,
Be this our battle call;
This lost, lost world for Jesus,
He well deserves it all.

118. All Around the World.

PRISCILLA J. OWENS. — E. S. LORENZ.

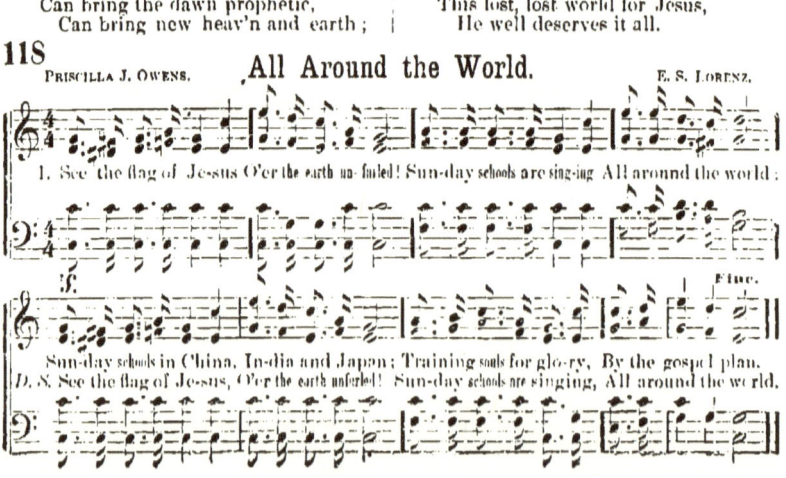

1. See the flag of Je-sus O'er the earth un-furled! Sun-day schools are sing-ing All around the world;

f.
Sun-day schools in China, In-dia and Japan; Training souls for glo-ry, By the gospel plan.
D. S. See the flag of Jesus, O'er the earth unfurled! Sun-day schools are singing, All around the world.

All Around the World. Concluded.

Lift the cross of Jesus, Bear the Bible on; Soon the world will echo, With his vict'ry won.

Used by permission of E. S. Lorenz, owner of the Copyright.

2 Little Indian diamonds,
Precious island pearls;
Learning Bible lessons,
Happy boys and girls.
Afric's gold dust scattered,
'Neath the feet of wrong;
Rises up in brightness,
From the darkness long.

3 Sunday schools are singing,
France and Spain and Rome;
Hear their joyous music,
Songs of heav'n and home.

Where the martyrs suffered,
Holy seed is spread;
Gather up these rubies,
Dyed in life-blood red.

4 Sunday schools in Chili,
Reaching down the coast;
Mexico is leading,
Gallant little host.
Glad Brazilian children,
Praise to God shall sing;
Far-off Patagonia
Answers Christ is King.

119   Cleave to the Saviour.
J. H. MARTIN, D. D.   R. M. McINTOSH.

Would you please and honor Jesus? Follow him in all you do; Would you win his love and fa-vor? Be his servant, faithful, true. Cleave to the Saviour day by day, Du-ty perform, and courage display, Tempted by sin, go seek him in pray'r; [Omit. . . . . . .] Cleave to the Saviour ev-'ry-where.

Copyright 1886, by R. M. McIntosh.

2 Would you have a friend in Jesus,
To support you in your way?
Own him as your Lord and Master,
Him receive, and love, obey.

3 Do you long to be with Jesus,
And a crown of life secure?
Be thou patient in his service,
Meekly to the end endure.

120. I Never Will Leave Thee.

E. A. Hoffman. — Elisha A. Hoffman.

O Jesus! I never will leave thee, For with thee, how bright is the way,
Without thee, how lone and how dreary! No, never from thee will I stray.

CHORUS.
No, never, no, never, No, never from thee will I stray, No, never, no, never, No, never from thee will I stray.

Copyright, 1882, by R. M. McIntosh.

2 My life would be desolate, cheerless,
Except for thy presence each day,
And so I will follow thee, fearless,
And never from thee will I stray

3 The world may despise and forsake me,
Their frowns can not turn me away;
My Saviour and friend have I made thee,
And never from thee will I stray.

121. The Saviour's Coming.

"The earth shall be full of his knowledge."

Mrs. M. B. C. Slade. — R. M. McIntosh, by per.

1. From all the dark places Of earth's heathen races, O, see how the thick shadows fly!

The voice of salvation Awakes ev'ry nation; Come over and help us, they cry.
D.S. The earth shall be full Of his knowledge and glory, As waters that cover the sea!

122. Work and Pray.

"Go work to-day."—MATT. 21: 28.   "Pray without ceasing."—1 THESS. 5: 17.

E. S. LORENZ.   E. S. LORENZ.

1. In this world of sin and woe Fee-ble ones are we; Yet we strive to do our best, Wea-ry ne'er to be. For we know that Je-sus smiles, When we him o-bey; Heed-ing his di-vine command, E'er to work and pray.

CHORUS.   Repeat softly.

Work and pray! work and pray! Till the toils of life are o-ver; And we rest with the blest, Safe on Je-sus' breast.

Used by permission of E. S. Lorenz, owner of the Copyright.

2 Idle must we never be,
Though our hands be frail;
If we ask for strength divine,
We can never fail.
Jesus' cause we should advance,
None should say him nay;
Every one must do his share,
All can work and pray.

3 Saviour, then in mercy look
On our little throng;
Let our prayers unceasing be,
And our efforts strong.
Help each one, so that in heaven,
When in white arrayed,
Full of gladness he may be,
That he worked and prayed.

The Saviour's Coming. Concluded.

CHORUS.   D. S.

The Saviour is coming; O, tell ye the sto-ry! God's ban-ner ex-alt-ed shall be!

2 The sunlight is glancing,
O'er armies advancing,
To conquer the kingdom of sin;
Our Lord shall possess them,
His presence shall bless them,
His beauty shall enter therein.

3 With shouting and singing,
And jubilant ringing,
Their arms of rebellion cast down;
At last every nation
The Lord of salvation
Their King and Redeemer shall crown.

123. His Love.

"The love of Christ, which passeth understanding."—Eph. 3: 19.

Mrs. L. K. Rogers. — Chas. H. Gabriel.

Go spread the joyful tidings Of his love, of his love, Tell the nations o'er the waters Of his love, of his love. Oh, the precious sto-ry, be mine the glo-ry To sound the blessed tidings of re-deeming love.

CHORUS.
The light is breaking, Jesus comes, Jesus comes, The light is breaking, Jesus comes, Jesus comes! Oh, precious sto-ry! be mine the glo-ry, To tell the blessed tidings of redeeming love.

Copyright 1890, by Chas. H. Gabriel. By per.

2 Tell those who mourn in darkness
  Of his love, of his love,
And repeat the blessed promise
  Of his love, of his love.
Oh, the precious story, replete with glory!
  Ring out the blessed tidings of redeeming love.

3 Fill all the world with praises
  Of his love, of his love,
Oh, how sweet to tell the story
  Of his love, of his love.
Yes, the precious story! be mine the glory
  To tell the blessed tidings of redeeming love.

124. Follow On!

W. O. Cushing. — Robert Lowry.

1. Down in the valley with my Savior I would go, Where the flow'rs are blooming and the sweet waters flow; Everywhere he leads me

Follow On! Concluded.

2 Down in the valley with my Saviour I would go,
Where the storms are sweeping and the dark waters flow;
With his hand to lead me, I will never, never fear:
Danger can not fright me if my Lord be near.

3 Down in the valley, or upon the mountain steep,
Close beside my Saviour would my soul ever keep;
He will lead me safely in the path that he hath trod,
Up to where they gather on the hills of God.

125 The Lord's Day.

H. R. PALMER.

2 Six days shalt thou toil,
Bringing fruits from the soil,
And with mind, heart and strength shalt thou labor;
But the seventh is blessed,
As a day of sweet rest,
And for worship of God, thy Creator.

3 O best of the seven,
Blessed foretaste of heaven
Thou dost bring with each pleasant returning;
Let us work, wait and pray,
Till the glorious day,
When we're called from life's weary sojourning.

126. Workers at Home.

DANIEL MARCH. ALEXANDER C. HOPKINS.

1. Hark the voice of Jesus calling—"Who will go and work to-day? Fields are white, the harvest waiting—Who will bear the sheaves a-way?" Loud and long the Master call-eth, Rich re-ward he of-fers free: Who will answer, glad-ly say-ing, "Here am I, O Lord: send me?" Who will an-swer, glad-ly say-ing, "Here am I, O Lord: send me?"

Copyright, 1887, by Fillmore Bros.

2 If you can not cross the ocean,
  And the heathen lands explore,
You can find the heathen nearer,
  You can help them at your door;
If you can not speak like angels,
  If you can not preach like Paul,
You can tell the love of Jesus,
  You can say he died for all.

3 While the souls of men are dying,
  And the Master calls for you,
Let none hear you idly saying,
  "There is nothing I can do."
Gladly take the task he gives you,
  Let his work your pleasure be;
Answer quickly when he calleth,
  "Here am I, O Lord: send me."

127. We'll Gather Them In.

E. A. HOFFMAN. R. M. McINTOSH.

1. We'll gather the children of want and sin Out of darkness and out of gloom; We'll bring them in joy to the Master's home; In his house there is ample room. We will gather them in to the feast of the King, From the

REFRAIN.

We'll Gather Them In. Concluded.

2 We'll gather them into the royal feast,
  Where the bounties of grace are spread;
  Where perishing souls with the bread of life
  In the tenderest love are fed.
3 We'll gather the halt, and the sick and blind,
  From the wearisome paths of sin,
  To Jesus, their Saviour and loving Friend,
  We will gather these lost ones in.
4 We'll gather the sad and the weary ones
  To the feet of the blessed Lord;
  He'll pardon their sin and renew their hearts;
  'Tis the hope of his precious word.

128 Only a Beam of Sunshine.

"Be kindly affectioned one to another."—Rom. 12: 10.

FANNY J. CROSBY.   JNO. R. SWENEY.

By per. John J. Hood.

2 Only a beam of sunshine
  That into a dwelling crept,
  Where over a fading rose-bud,
  A mother her vigil kept.
  Only a beam of sunshine
  That smiled through her falling tears,
  And show'd her the bow of promise,
  Forgotten, perhaps, for years.

3 Only a word for Jesus!
  Oh, speak it in his dear name;
  To perishing souls around you
  The message of love proclaim.
  Go, like the faithful sunbeam,
  Your mission of joy fulfill,
  Remember the Saviour's promise,
  That he will be with you still.

129. Gather Them into the Fold.

 M. A. KIDDER.   "Come, for all things are ready."—LUKE 14: 17.    W. A. OGDEN.

1. O-pen the door for the chil-dren, Ten-der-ly gath-er them in, In from the highways and hedges, In from the plac-es of sin. Some are so young and so help-less, Some are so hun-gry and cold;

CHORUS.
O-pen the door for the chil-dren, Gath-er them in-to the fold. Gath - er them in, . . Gather them in, O, gather them in, Gath - er them in; Gath-er, O gath-er them in; O - pen the door for the chil-dren, Gath-er them in-to the fold.

From "Crown of Life," by permission of W. W. Whitney.

2 Open the door for the children,
See! they are coming in throngs,
Bid them sit down to the banquet,
Teach them your beautiful songs.
Pray you the Father to bless them,
Pray you that grace may be given;
Open the door for the children,
"Of such is the kingdom of heaven."

3 Open the door for the children,
Take the dear lambs by the hand;
Point them to truth and to Jesus,
Point them to heaven's bright land.
Some are so young and so helpless,
Some are so hungry and cold;
Open the door for the children,
Gather them into the fold.

130. God Speed the Right.

W. E. HIRKSON.   From the German.

1. { Now to heav'n our pray'rs ascending, God speed the right;
   In a no-ble cause contending, God speed the right; } Be our zeal in heav'n recorded,

Free Giving.

MRS. M. B. C. SLADE. "The Lord loveth a cheerful giver." R. M. MCINTOSH, by per.

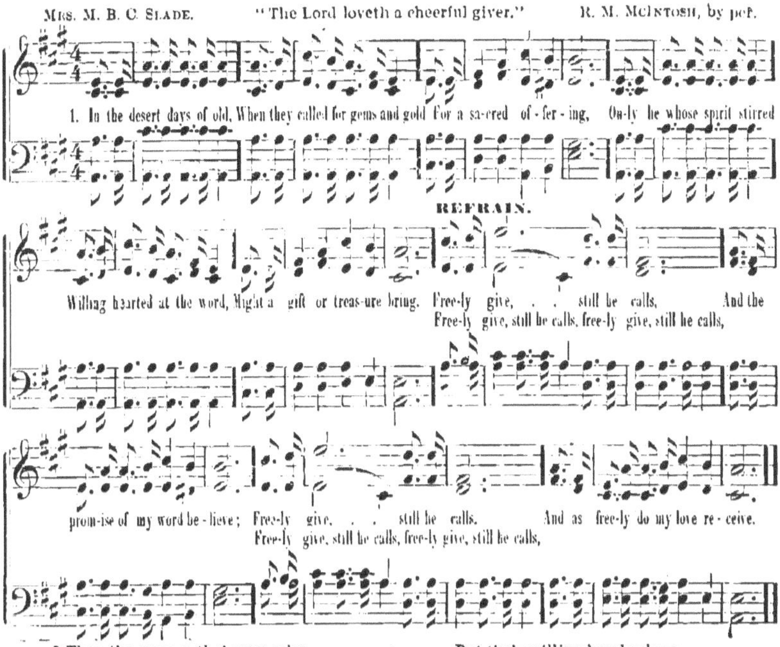
1. In the desert days of old, When they called for gems and gold For a sa-cred of-fer-ing, On-ly he whose spirit stirred
REFRAIN.
Willing hearted at the word, Might a gift or treas-ure bring. Free-ly give, . . still he calls, And the
Free-ly give, still he calls, free-ly give, still he calls,
prom-ise of my word be-lieve; Free-ly give, . . still he calls. And as free-ly do my love re-ceive.
Free-ly give, still he calls, free-ly give, still he calls,

2 Then the women that were wise,
Spun of blue and purple dyes,
And the call was heard by them;
But by willing hands alone
Might the 'broidery work be done
Of the sacred vesture hem.

3 Mighty rulers came and gave
Shining gems whereon to 'grave
All the names of Israel;
But their willing hands alone,
With the precious onyx-stone,
Might the needful treasure swell.

4 Thus the work of God's command,
By his holy prophet's hand,
Was in sacred service wrought;
But the best and blessed part
Was the glad and willing heart
That his loving children brought.

God Speed the Right. Concluded.

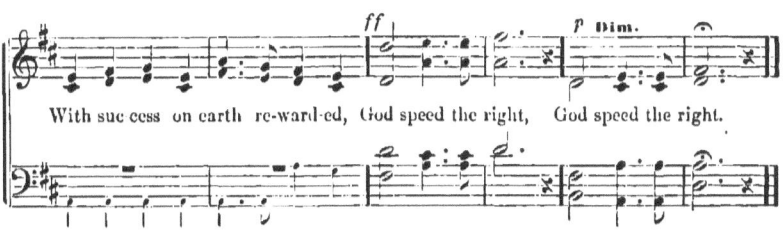

ff
p Dim.
With suc-cess on earth re-ward-ed, God speed the right, God speed the right.

1 Now to heav'n our prayers ascending,
God speed the right;
In a noble cause contending,
God speed the right;
Be our zeal in heav'n recorded,
With success on earth rewarded,
‖: God speed the right. :‖

2 Be that pray'r again repeated,
God speed the right;
Ne'er despairing though defeated,
God speed the right;
Like the good and great in story,
If we fail, we fail with glory,
‖: God speed the right. :‖

3 Patient, firm, and persevering,
God speed the right;
Ne'er th' event nor danger fearing,
God speed the right;
Pains, nor toils, nor trials heeding,
And in heav'n's own time succeeding,
‖: God speed the right. :‖

4 Still our onward course pursuing,
God speed the right;
Ev'ry foe at length subduing,
God speed the right;
Truth our cause, whate'er delay it,
There's no power on earth can stay it;
‖: God speed the right. :‖

134. The Rock and the Sand.

H. R. TRICKETT. MATT. 7: 21, 27. J. H. ROSECRANS, by per.

1. On what are you building, my brother, Your hopes of an e-ter-nal home? Is it loose, shifting sand, or the firm, sol-id rock, You are trusting for a-ges to come?

CHORUS.

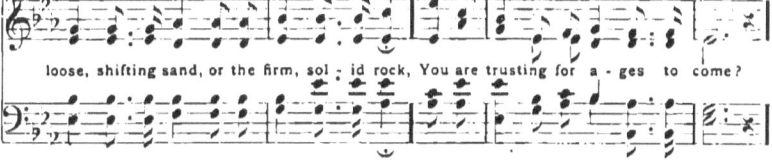

Hear-ing and do-ing, we build on the Rock; Hear-ing a-lone, we build on the sand;

Both will be tried by the storm and the flood—On-ly the Rock the tri-al will stand.

2 On one or the other, my brother,
 You are building your hopes, day by day;
 You are risking your soul on the works that you do;
 Will the dark waters sweep you away?

3 Your Saviour has warned you, my brother;
 I pray you, give heed to his voice;
 There is life on the rock, but there's death on the sand—
 O, my brother, pray tell me your choice.

4 No matter how careful, my brother,
 The sand for your house you prepare,
 'Twill be all swept away when the floods shall descend,
 Leaving nothing but death and despair.

Let Them Come. Concluded.

2 When the mothers came and brought him
 Tender infants, young and small,
 And so earnestly besought him
 For his blessing on them all.

3 Though disciples would rebuke them,
 Turn the little ones away,
 In his gentle arms he took them,
 And they heard him sweetly say:

4 Little children, now from Jesus,
 Will you his dear blessing seek?
 From his home on high he sees us,
 Hear him kindly to us speak.

5 Just as close his arms will hold you;
 Just as kind his blessings fall;
 Just as warm his love enfold you,
 Just as sweetly doth he call.

2 O, tell me once more of his wonderful love,
His goodness and mercy to me!
When hopelessly lost in the darkness of sin,
He found me and bade me go free.

3 O, tell me again of the land of the blest,
Where sorrow and sin never come!
Where I with the Saviour shall evermore dwell,
O, tell me of heaven, my home!

136 Remember, Jesus Leads.

WM. J. KIRKPATRICK.

1. Ye followers of Christ, go forth, Your Master's call obey;
   Stay not till all the tribes of earth Shall own his sov'reign sway;
   Go, seek the souls that erring stray,
   For them a Saviour pleads, And while you keep the narrow way,
   Remember Jesus leads.

CHORUS.
Remember, remember, Remember Jesus leads;
Who trust in him are blest, He leads to perfect rest;
O, remember Jesus leads, Jesus leads!

2 His faithful ones who ever strive
 His righteous cause to win,
Shall see their Master's work revive,
 His vict'ry over sin.
A fallen world in darkness lies,
 Each to the rescue speeds,
Though foes on every side arise,
 Remember, Jesus leads.

3 Go up against sin's fortress walls
 Go in the strength of grace;
And if a standard bearer falls,
 Then you must take his place.
O, tell his love that can not fail!
 Make known his glorious deeds;
And tho' you walk thro' death's dark vale,
 Remember, Jesus leads.

137. Then Hoist the Sails.

S. WESLEY MARTIN.

1. What vessel are you sailing in, While on the voyage of life?
Our vessel is the ark of God, "The way, the truth, the life."
2. Our compass is the "Word of God," Our anchor, steadfast hope;
The love of God fills ev-'ry sail, And faith's our anchor rope.

And what's the port your sailing for, What calm and peaceful bay?
The port is New Je - ru-sa-lem, The realms of endless day.
How ma-ny have you now on board That no-ble ship di-vine?
Ten thousand thousand happy souls, And room for all mankind.

CHORUS.
Then hoist the sails To catch the gale, Each sailor ply the oar, The night begins to wear away, We soon shall reach the shore.

*Select two Duets,—Let the 1st Duet sing the 1st, 2d, 5th and 6th lines of the 1st stanza, and the 2d Duet sing the 3d, 4th, 7th and 8th lines. Of the 2d stanza, the 1st Duet sings only the 5th and 6th lines, and the 2d Duet sing the 1st, 2d, 3d, 4th, 7th and 8th lines.

138. Gather Them In.

"Go out into the highways and hedges, and compel them to come in."—LUKE 14: 23.

FANNY J. CROSBY.   GEO. C. STEBBINS.

1. Gather them in, for there yet is room At the feast that a King has spread; O gather them in, let his house be filled, And the hungry and poor be fed.

CHORUS.
Out in the highway, out in the by-way, Out in the dark depths of sin, Go forth, go forth with a loving heart, And gather the wand'rers in.

Copyright, 1883, by Geo. C. Stebbins, used by permission.

2 Gather them in, for there yet is room;
But our hearts, how they throb with pain,
To think of the many who slight the call
That may never be heard again.

3 Gather them in, for there yet is room;
'T is a message from God above:
O, gather them in to the fold of grace,
And the arms of the Saviour's love.

139 We're Coming, Dear Saviour.

I. B.   "Him that cometh to me I will in no wise cast out."—JOHN 6: 6.   I. BALTZELL, by per.

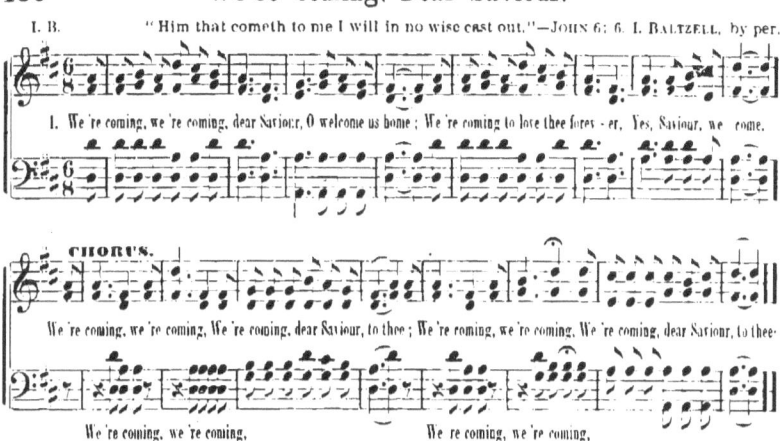

2 We're coming, we're coming, dear Saviour,
   To meet the glad band;
To sing hallelujah forever
   With them, in that land.

3 We're coming, we're coming, dear Saviour,
   Thy glory to see;

A home with thy children forever,
   Give, Saviour, to me.

4 We're coming to tell the glad story
   To Jesus, our King;
And then, with the children in glory,
   His praises we'll sing.

140 Follow Me.

M. B. SLEIGHT.   "And they left all."   H. R. PALMER.

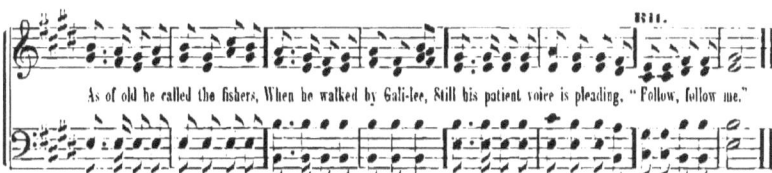

Used by permission of H. R. Palmer, owner of the Copyright.

2 Who will heed the holy mandate?
   "Follow me, follow me!"
Leaving all things at his bidding?
   "Follow, follow me!"
Hark! that tender voice entreating
   Mariners on life's rough sea,
Gently, lovingly repeating,
   "Follow, follow me!"

3 Hearken, lest he plead no longer,
   "Follow me, follow me!"
Once again, O hear him calling,
   "Follow, follow me!"
Turning swift at thy sweet summons,
   Evermore, O Christ, would we,
For thy love all else forsaking,
   Follow, follow thee!

141. We are Coming.

Mrs. H. E. Brown.   W. A. Ogden.

2 We are kneeling, we are kneeling,
   Here together at thy feet,
Cheerful vows of service sealing,
   Strength to keep them we entreat.
Little pilgrims are we, starting
   On a rough and dangerous way;
Grace in all our need imparting,
   Hold us, Jesus, here we pray.

3 We are singing, we are singing
   Songs of gladness as we pass;
For thy love, in us distilling
   Like the showers upon the grass;
For the home in heaven preparing
   To receive our weary feet;
For thy smiles, our pathway cheering,
   Songs of praises we repeat.

4 We are running, we are running,
   Dearest Saviour, after thee;
Show to us the way thou 'rt going;
   All thy footprints make us see.
We are very weak and sinful,
   Easily enticed astray;
Satan watches for our halting;
   Keep, O keep us in the way.

5 We are coming, we are coming,
   Speeding onward to thy throne,
Where in majesty thou 'rt waiting,—
   Waiting to receive thine own.
Out of every tribe and nation,
   We are gathering at thy call,
For thy glorious coronation,
   Jesus, Saviour, Lord of all.

142. Work Song.

ANNA L. WALKER. — LOWELL MASON.

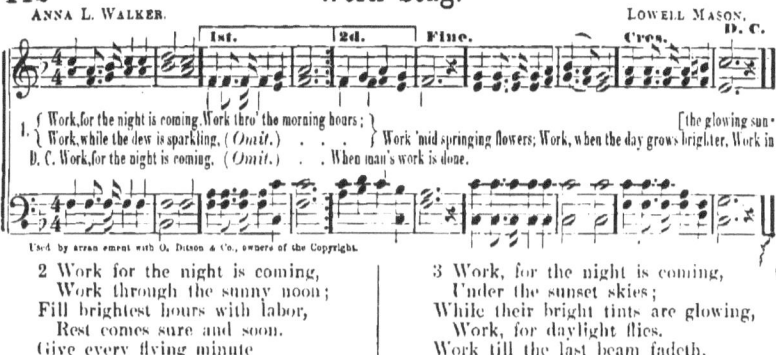

1. Work, for the night is coming, Work thro' the morning hours;
Work, while the dew is sparkling, (Omit.) . . . Work 'mid springing flowers; Work, when the day grows brighter, Work in
D. C. Work, for the night is coming, (Omit.) . . . When man's work is done. [the glowing sun

Used by arrangement with O. Ditson & Co., owners of the Copyright.

2 Work for the night is coming,
Work through the sunny noon;
Fill brightest hours with labor,
Rest comes sure and soon.
Give every flying minute
Something to keep in store;
Work, for the night is coming,
When man works no more.

3 Work, for the night is coming,
Under the sunset skies;
While their bright tints are glowing,
Work, for daylight flies.
Work till the last beam fadeth,
Fadeth to shine no more;
Work while the night is darkening,
When man's work is o'er.

143. Dare to do Right.

CHAS. H. GABRIEL.

Dare to think, tho' others frown; Dare in words your tho'ts express; Dare to rise, tho' oft cast down;

CHORUS.

Dare the wronged and scorned to bless. Do what con-science says is right, Do what
Do what conscience says is right,

rea - son says is best, Do with all your mind and heart, Do your du - ty and be blest.
Do what reason says is best, Do with all your mind and heart, Do your duty and be blest.

Copyright, 1890, by Chas. H. Gabriel.

2 Dare from custom to depart;
Dare the priceless pearl possess;
Dare to wear it next your heart;
Dare, when others curse, to bless.

3 Dare forsake what you deem wrong;
Dare to walk in wisdom's way;
Dare to give where gifts belong;
Dare God's precepts to obey.

144. Following Jesus.

Mrs. M. B. C. Slade. — Dr. A. B. Everett.

1. If I, like Gal-i-lee fish-ers, Were mending my nets by the main, And Jesus, coming, should call me, He never should call in vain.

CHORUS.
We'll follow the summons of Jesus, Wherever, however it falls; When high up the pathway he sees us, And "Follow thou me!" he calls.

2 If I were dwelling in pleasure,
  Or sitting in places of gain,
  And Jesus, passing, should call me,
  He never should call in vain.

3 If I were sinking in sadness,
  Or dreading the cross and the pain,
  And Jesus tenderly called me,
  He never should call in vain.

145. Lambs of Jesus.

"He shall feed his flock like a shepherd; he shall gather the lambs with his arm."—Isa. 40. 11.

Dr. C. R. Blackall. — E. S. Lorenz.

1. We are the lambs, and Je-sus is our Shep-herd, If we his coun-sel fol-low and o-bey, Close in his arms may lov-ing-ly be fold-ed, Guid-ed when-e'er we do not know the way.

CHORUS.
Where he leads, we will fol-low, Where he leads, we will fol-low, We will follow the good Shepherd all the way, (all the way;)

Used by permission of E. S. Lorenz, owner of the Copyright.

Lambs of Jesus. Concluded.

2 We may be kind and gentle as the Shepherd,
   All he has taught us gladly we may do;
   Trusting in him no trial e'er shall move us,
   He is our strength, and he is ever true.

3 We are the lambs, O, how we love the Shepherd!
   When all our heart to him is truly given,
   Joyfully then we follow where he leadeth,
   And we obtain a foretaste here of heaven.

146   Growing Up for Jesus.

PRISCILLA J. OWENS.   WM. J. KIRKPATRICK.

Copyright, 1885, by WM. J. KIRKPATRICK.

2 Not too young to love him, little hearts beat true,
   Not too young to serve him, as the dew-drops do,
   Not too young to praise him, singing as we come,
   Not too young to answer when he calls us home.

3 Growing up for Jesus, learning day by day
   How to follow onward in the narrow way;
   Seeking holy treasure, finding precious truth,
   Growing up for Jesus in our happy youth.

147. Satan the Seed is Sowing.

1. Satan the seed is sow-ing— So ear-nest-ly sow-ing, sowing—Tares with the wheat are grow-ing, To-geth-er grow-ing here And the an-gels will gather, By and by— by and by— The tares for the burning, And the wheat for the sky! The an-gels will gather, By and by— by and by— The tares for the burning, And the wheat for the sky!

2 God for the wheat is caring—
So tenderly caring, caring—
Though till the harvest sparing
The tares which now appear.

3 Souls are the wheat he's keeping—
So lovingly keeping, keeping—

Safe for the time of reaping,
And garners built above.

4 Harvest the tares will sever—
Eternally sever, sever—
Then may we be forever
Safe in the Master's love.

148. We Shall Reap By and By.

FANNY CROSBY.   "Let us not be weary in well doing."—GAL. 6: 9.   A. J. ABBEY.

1. O nev-er be weary, with vig-or pur-sue The work which the Master has left us to do: If pa-tient-ly toiling we trust in the Lord, The harvest will bring us a blessed reward. We shall reap if we faint not, reap by and by, Treasures im-

We Shall Reap By and By. Concluded.

2 O never be weary, but work with a will,
Our Father will surely his promise fulfill;
From seeds we have scattered in sorrow and tears
We'll gather bright sheaves when the harvest appears.

3 O never be weary, through trial and care;
Be faithful to duty and earnest in prayer;
No labor for Jesus was ever in vain;
Go work in his vineyard, and wait for the rain.

4 Remember his mercy, remember his love,
Who came, our Redeemer, from glory above;
Then never be weary, but joyf'lly pursue
The work which the Master has left us to do.

149 Sowing and Reaping.

K. Shaw.   "They that sow in tears, shall reap in joy."   Geo. A. Minor.

2 Go and tell the nations now in heathen blindness,
Tell them Jesus died—now no excuse he leaves;
Bid them come to Jesus, thus prepare the harvest,
You shall come rejoicing, bringing in the sheaves.

3 Sowing in the sunshine, sowing in the shadows,
Fearing neither clouds nor winter's chilling breeze;
By and by the harvest and our labors ended,
We shall come rejoicing, bringing in the sheaves.

4 Go, then, even weeping, sowing for the Master,
Though the loss sustained our spirit often grieves,
When our weeping's over, he will bid us welcome,
We shall come rejoicing, bringing in the sheaves.

2 We'll follow where he leadeth,
We'll pasture where he feedeth,
We'll yield to him who pleadeth
   From on high.
Then naught from him shall sever,
Our hopes shall brighten ever,
And faith shall fail us never,
   He is nigh.

3 Our home is bright above us,
No trials dark to move us,
But Jesus dear to love us
   There on high;
We'll give him best endeavor,
And praise his name forever;
His precious words can never,
   Never die.

151. How to Win.

LANTA WILSON SMITH. S. F. ACKLEY.

1 If you feel a love for sinners,
  Do not cold and idle stand,
  Though you have no words to utter,
  You can reach a friendly hand.
  Give a grasp that's kind and earnest,
  It will surely reach the heart,
  It may help some friendless wand'rer,
  To accept the better part.

2 Never look upon the sinner
  With a cold and scornful eye;
  Just remember what compassion
  Jesus showed in days gone by.
  Let your glance be kind and winning,
  Let it show the love you feel
  For the sinful ones that Jesus
  Came to bless, and save, and heal.

THE WORDS OF JESUS.

"Sanctify them through thy truth, Thy Word is Truth."—Jno. 17:17.

155   The Wonderful Word.

MRS. W. M. BELL.   J. F. KINSEY.

I nev-er open the precious book, But what to my wandering mind, Vast treasures of beauty and wealth unfold, From my heaven-ly Fa-ther kind. And when it is dark, and I can not see The path my feet should tread, I turn to the Bible and light breaks forth, And glory shines 'round my head. So I'll trust in the wonderful word, I'll trust in the wonder-ful, won-der-ful word, That when I am done with this world of care, I shall en-ter the rest of heav'n.

2 The bread of heaven is offered me,
  Of which I may eat and live ;
The fountain of water to quench my thirst,
  Which our Father above can give.
The righteousness which I must have
  If the crown would win ;
The favor to help me from day to day,
  To separate me from sin.

3 And when we turn from our toil away,
  To study the sacred page,
We gather a lesson for each of us
  For the cleansing of youth and age.
Oh, may it shape and mould our lives,
  That we may win in the strife ;
And when we reach home we will thank the Lord
  For the wonderful word of life.

156. The Blessed Book.

"My tongue shall speak of thy word."

Tom C. Neal.

1. There's a book which sur-pass-es the sa-ges, A vol-ume of wis-dom di-vine;
And the glo-ry that gleams from its pa-ges, No splen-dor of earth can out-shine.

CHORUS.
'Tis the Bi - - - ble! the Bi - - - ble! our
'Tis the bless-ed, bless-ed Bi-ble! the bless-ed, bless-ed Bi-ble! Our
guid-ing star that leads from earth to heaven! The Bi - - - ble! the
The blessed, blessed Bi-ble! the
Bi - - - ble! We love the precious Book of Truth which God has given.
blessed, blessed Bi-ble! We

2 'T is the light which will guide us to glory,
The sword of the spirit of might;
And to dwell on its beautiful story,
Is of heaven the sweetest delight.

3 It reveals where a fountain is flowing,
Which washes the soul from its stain;
Age and sorrow are comforted, knowing
With earth they shall part with all pain.

157. The Golden Rule.

1 The golden rule, the golden rule,
  Oh, that's the law for me;
  Were this the law for all the world,
  How happy we should be.

2 Were this the rule, in harmony
  Our lives would pass away;
  And none would suffer, none be poor,
  And none their trust betray.

CHORUS.—The golden rule, the golden rule,
  Oh, that's the law for me;
  To do to others as I would
  That they should do to me.

158. The Living Water.

Mrs. HARRIET JONES. JOHN 4: 14. D. B. TOWNER.

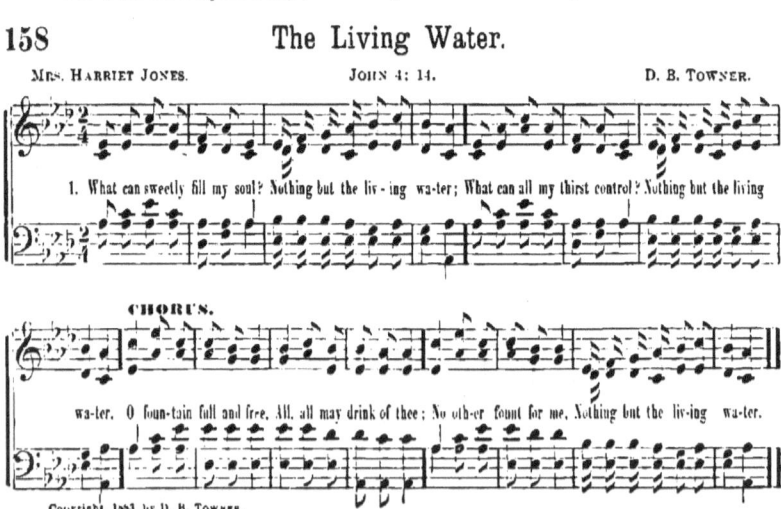

Copyright, 1883, by D. B. Towner.

159. Precious Words.

"The gospel is the power of God unto salvation."

MRS. LOULA K. ROGERS. R. M. McINTOSH, by per.

1. Pre-cious for-ev-er, O, won-der-ful words, Teach me the path-way of du-ty;
Lead me be-side the still wa-ters of life, Flow-ing thro' val-leys of beau-ty.

REFRAIN.
Pre-cious for-ev-er to you and to me, Words that our Saviour has spok-en,
Bear-ing sal-va-tion far o-ver the sea, Healing the hearts that are brok-en!

2 Freely he offers their promise to all,
  "Come unto me whosoever,"
Sinners oppressed with a burden of woe,
  Drink of the bountiful river.

3 Wouldst thou refuse the sweet solace he gives,
  In the midnight of thy sorrow?
Wouldst thou go on in the darkness of sin,
  Longing for no bright to-morrow?

The Living Water. Concluded.

2 Clear as crystal from the throne,
  Nothing but the living water;
Sweetly filling all his own,
  Nothing but the living water.

3 Pure and brimming to the brink,
  Nothing but the living water;
Whosoever will may drink,
  Nothing but the living water.

4 Come, my brother, and partake,
  Nothing but the living water;
Drink, O drink, for Jesus' sake,
  Nothing but the living water.

5 Fountain open now for thee,
  Nothing but the living water;
Come, O come, and drink with me,
  Nothing but the living water.

160. Give Me the Bible. 11s & 10s.

P. J. Owens. E. S. Lorenz.

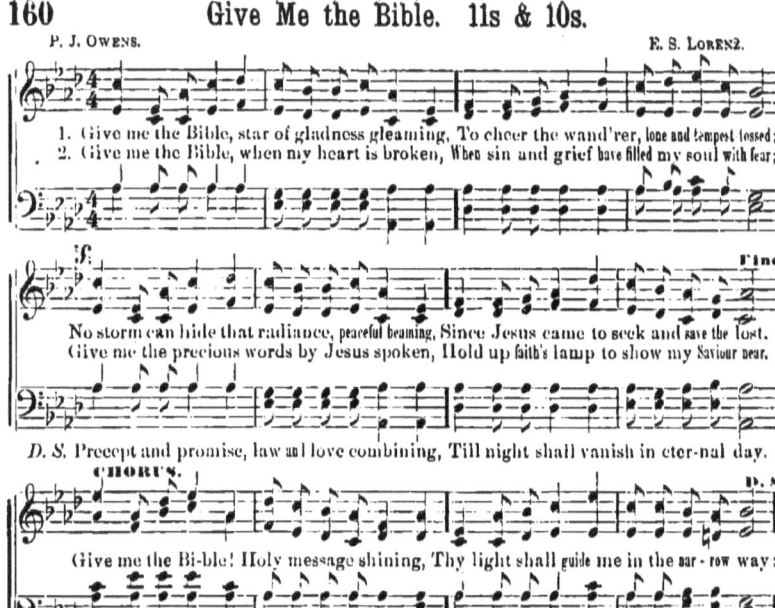

1. Give me the Bible, star of gladness gleaming, To cheer the wand'rer, lone and tempest tossed;
No storm can hide that radiance, peaceful beaming, Since Jesus came to seek and save the lost.

2. Give me the Bible, when my heart is broken, When sin and grief have filled my soul with fear;
Give me the precious words by Jesus spoken, Hold up faith's lamp to show my Saviour near.

D. S. — Precept and promise, law and love combining, Till night shall vanish in eternal day.

CHORUS.

Give me the Bi-ble! Holy message shining, Thy light shall guide me in the nar-row way:

3 Give me the Bible, all my steps enlighten,
Teach me the danger of these realms below,
That lamp of safety, o'er the gloom shall brighten,
That light alone, the path of peace can show.

4 Give me the Bible, lamp of life immortal,
Hold up that splendor by the open grave;
Show me the light from heaven's shining portal,
Show me the glory gilding Jordan's wave.

161. Precious Bible.

Joseph Irons. Wm. F. Sherwin.

1. Precious Bi-ble, what a store For the sons of men t'explore; Precious Christ, it speaks of thee; Give us eyes thy-self to see. Pre-cious Bi-ble, pre-cious Bi-ble, God's own Word of love to me.

Pre-cious Bi-ble, Pre-cious Bi-ble,

162. Blessed Words.

E. A. HOFFMAN. Ps. 119: 105. Prov. 6: 21—23 inclusive. E. S. LORENZ.

Copyright, 1889, by E. S. Lorenz.

2 Blessed words of life and light! shining clearly in the night
Of temptation and of sorrow,
Tho' the sky be overcast, bringing hope to dawn at last,
Making beautiful and radiant the morrow.

3 Oh, the blessed Word of Truth! I will love it in my youth,
Keep it near me, ever near me;
It will nerve me for the right, it will bring me peace and light,
And amid my daily toils it will cheer me.

Precious Bible. Concluded.

2 Precious Bible, what a friend,
All my footsteps to attend;
All my wants it can supply,
For it brings my Saviour nigh.

3 Precious Bible, what a field!
Richest fruit its furrows yield;
Wide extent and fertile ground,
Verdant pastures here are found.

4 Precious Bible, what a mine!
Full of promises divine;
I would all thy wealth explore,
And thy Author, God, adore.

163. Wonderful Words For All.

F. M. Davis. Frank M. Davis.

2 Wonderful words to the weary;
Come, heavy laden ones, come
You shall find rest, saith the spirit,
Rest in my heavenly home.

3 Wonderful words, to the seeker;
Ask in my name, and receive;
Joy and salvation awaits you,
If you on me will believe.

164. In the Blessed Bible.

O. D. Sherman. J. M. Stillman.

165. There's a Light in the Bible.

W. H. W. W. H. WONDER.

1. There's a light in the Bi-ble for me, Yes, for me, in the Book, I am told;
O, the light of its love in its richness I see, As in faith I its pa-ges un-fold.

CHORUS.
There's a light in the Bi-ble, That will shine thro' the valley of death;
There's a light in the Bible, there's a light for all,
There's a light in the Bi-ble That will shine thro' the valley of death.
There's a light in the Bible, there's a light for all,

2 There's a light in the Bible for thee,
With a beautiful, beautiful beam;
'T is the light for thy way that its dangers may flee,
O, then, catch its bright, beautiful gleam!

3 There's a light in the Bible for all,
It is beaming, all-loving and kind;
It will scatter the gloom of the doubts that enthrall,
'T is the promise, who seek it shall find.

In the Blessed Bible. Concluded.

2 Would you know his artless childhood,
Free from sin and wicked strife,
Full of smiles and loving favor,
Brave and truthful in his life?
Read the Bible, blessed Bible,
Read its pages all you can;
It will tell you how he labored,
Loving God and blessing man.

3 Would you hear his words of wisdom,
See the glory of his face;
How he blessed the little children,
Held them in his close embrace?

In the Bible, precious Bible,
All this matchless love appears;
How he healed the broken-hearted,
How he dried the mourner's tears.

4 Would you know how dark that garden,
Terraced on the mountain side?
Would you know the taunts and jeerings;
See the cross on which he died?
Read your Bible, precious Bible;
All the story you may know,
And the price of man's redemption,
Saved from sin and endless woe.

166. Treasures.

"Out of the mouth of babes and sucklings thou hast perfected praise."—MATT. 21:16.

C. J. WEBB.

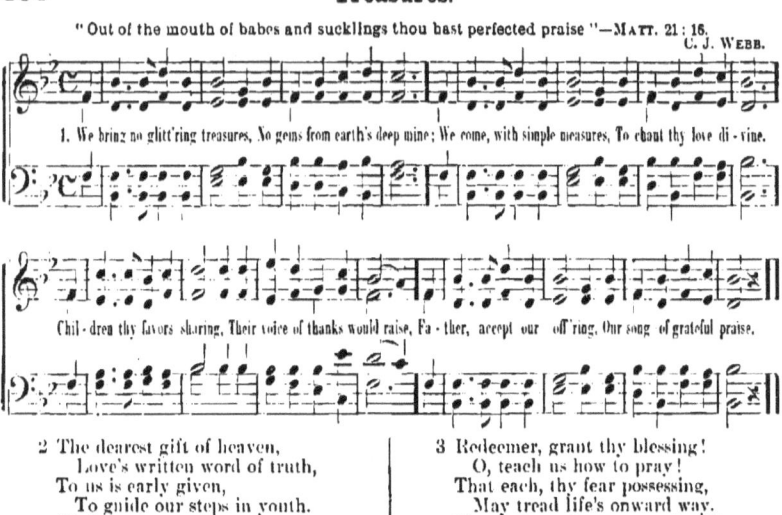

1. We bring no glitt'ring treasures, No gems from earth's deep mine; We come, with simple measures, To chant thy love divine. Chil-dren thy favors sharing, Their voice of thanks would raise, Fa-ther, accept our off'ring, Our song of grateful praise.

2 The dearest gift of heaven,
   Love's written word of truth,
 To us is early given,
   To guide our steps in youth.
 We hear the wondrous story,
   The tale of Calvary;
 We read of homes in glory,
   From sin and sorrow free.

3 Redeemer, grant thy blessing!
   O, teach us how to pray!
 That each, thy fear possessing,
   May tread life's onward way.
 Then, where the pure are dwelling,
   We'll hope to meet again;
 And, sweeter numbers swelling,
   Forever praise thy name.

167. "Book of Grace."

"Thy word is truth."—JOHN 17:17.

W. B. BRADBURY.

1. Book of grace and book of glo-ry, Gift of God to age and youth, Won-drous is thy sa-cred sto-ry, Bright, bright with truth. Won-drous is thy sa-cred sto-ry, Bright, bright with truth.

2 Book of love! in accents tender
   Speaking unto such as we;
 May it lead us, Lord, to render
   All, all to thee.

3 Book of hope! the spirit, sighing,
   Sweetest comfort finds in thee,
 As it hears the Saviour crying,
   "Come, come to me!"

4 Book of peace! when nights of sorrow
   Fall upon us drearily,
 Thou wilt bring a shining morrow,
   Full, full of thee.

5 Book of life! when we, reposing,
   Bid farewell to friends we love,
 Give us, for the life then closing,
   Life, life above.

168. Drink and Live.

"Ho! every one that thirsteth, come ye to the water."

C. H. Gabriel. — E. S. Lorenz.

2 Hark to the invitation God gives you,
  Drink, and ye shall be thirsty no more;
  Come, lest ye perish, why are ye waiting?
  Come, O ye weary, thirsty, and poor!

3 Come, whosoever will, to the fountain,
  Come without money, come ye and drink;
  Jesus invites you, why do you tarry?
  'Tis but a step from you to the brink.

169. Searching the Scriptures.

"Search the scriptures; for in them ye think ye have eternal life."—JOHN 5: 39.

JOHN JUNKIN FRANCIS.   W. A. OGDEN.

1. We are searching the scriptures, God's blessed word of truth, We are seek-ing his sal-va-tion, In the sun-ny days of youth; Seeking more to know of Je-sus, Who for us was cru-ci-fied, Knowing they and on-ly they, are safe, Who in his truth a-bide.

CHORUS. Loud.

Wiser, purer, better would we grow, Learning more of Jesus Ev'ry day, as on we go; Seek-ing his sal-va-tion, In the sun-ny days of youth; Searching the scriptures, God's bless-ed word of truth.

2 We are searching the scriptures:
They tell us of his love,
And they point us in the way that leads
To yon bright heaven above;
As we daily grow in knowledge,
May we also grow in grace,
Letting ever our light shine around us,
Each one in his place.

3 We are searching the scriptures:
Lord, make us truly wise;
From our minds dispel the darkness,
Saviour, open thou our eyes;
Help us to obey thy precepts,
Taught us in thy holy word;
Help us more and more to be like thee,
Our Master and our Lord.

170. Thank God for the Bible.

"Thy word was unto me the joy and rejoicing of mine heart."—JER. 15: 16.

ANON.
I. BALTZELL, by per.

1. Thank God for the Bi-ble! 'tis here that we find The sto-ry of Christ and his love— How he came down to earth from his beau-ti-ful home In the man-sions of glo-ry a-bove. Thank God for the Bi-ble! the dear, bless-ed Bi-ble! The vol-ume that guid-ed my youth; And its truth I'll proclaim, while in death I'll exclaim, Thank God for the Bi-ble of truth.

2 Thank God for the Bible! 'tis here that we read
Of Jesus, the Son that was given;
How he said, suffer children to come unto me,
For of such is the kingdom of heaven.

3 Thank God for the Bible! it tells of a land
Where sorrow and pain are all o'er;
Where the Saviour has gone to prepare us a home,
In the beautiful, bright evermore.

4 Thank God for the Bible! its truth o'er the earth
We'll sow with a bountiful hand;
But we never can tell what the Bible is worth,
Till we go to that beautiful land.

TEMPERANCE SONGS.

"Every man that striveth for the mastery is temperate in all things."—1 Cor. 9 : 25.

175   We'll Crown Them.

"Bring them up."   W. A. OGDEN.

1. We'll take up our stand for the youth of our land, And weave them a gar-land to wear;
Though no leaves of the vine in our wreath shall entwine, For we'll crown them with ros-es so fair.

CHORUS.
We'll crown them, we'll crown them, We'll crown them with ros-es so fair;
We'll crown them with ros-es, we'll crown them with ros-es,
We'll crown them, we'll crown them, We'll crown them with ros-es to wear.
We'll crown them with ros-es, we'll crown them with ros-es,

By permission of W. W. Whitney.

2 We'll tempt not the youth from the fountain of truth,
Whose waters are pure and divine,
But we'll banish fore'er from our homes that are dear,
The chalice that sparkles with wine.

3 Our sweet household joys, the girls and the boys,
We'll shield from the tempter so bold;
And we'll bind their white brows that with innocence glow,
With a crown that is richer than gold.

176 Looking to Jesus.

H. R. PALMER. "The Lord knoweth how to deliver." H. R. PALMER.

1. Yield not to temp-ta-tion, For yielding is sin, Each vic-t'ry will help us Some oth-er to win; Fight man-ful-ly on-ward, Dark pas-sions sub-due, Look ev-er to Je-sus, He'll car-ry you through.

CHORUS.
Ask the Saviour to help you, Comfort, strengthen and keep you; He is willing to aid you, He will carry you through.

Used by permission of H. R. Palmer, owner of the Copyright.

2 Shun evil companions,
   Bad language disdain,
 God's name hold in rev'rence,
   Nor take it in vain;
 Be thoughtful and earnest,
   Kind-hearted and true,
 Look ever to Jesus,
   He'll carry you through.

3 To him that o'ercometh,
   God giveth a crown,
 Through faith we shall conquer,
   Though often cast down;
 He who is our Saviour
   Our strength will renew,
 Look ever to Jesus,
   He'll carry you through.

177 Dare to Do Right.

W. B. BRADBURY.

1. Dare to do right! Dare to be true! You have a work that no other can do, Do it so bravely, so kind-ly, so well,

CHORUS. Rit.
Angels will hasten the story to tell. Dare, dare, dare to do right, Dare, dare, dare to be true, Dare to be true, Dare to be true! Dare,

Used by permission of The Biglow & Main Co., owners of the Copyright.

2 Dare to do right! Dare to be true!
Other men's failures can never save you;
Stand by your conscience, your honor, your faith,
Stand like a hero, and battle till death.

3 Dare to do right! Dare to be true!
God, who created you, cares for you too:
Treasures the tears that his striving ones shed,
Counts and protects every hair of your head.

4 Dare to do right! Dare to be true!
Keep the great judgment-seat always in view;
Look at your work as you'll look at it then—
Scanned by Jehovah, and angels, and men.

5 Dare to do right! Dare to be true!
Jesus, your Saviour, will carry you through;
City, and mansion, and throne all in sight,
Can you not dare to be true and do right?

178. The Sweetest Draught.

Music by T. F. SEWARD. From *Temple Choir*, by per.

1. Come, let us sing of fount and spring, Of brook-let, stream and riv-er, And tune our praise to him al-ways, The great and gra-cious Giv-er.

CHORUS. What drink with wa-ter can compare, That nat-ure loves so dearly? The sweetest draught that can be quaffed Is water, (water), water, (water), water that sparkles so clear-ly.

2 Down fall the showers to feed the flowers,
And in the summer, nightly,
The blossoms sip with rosy lip
The dewdrops gleaming brightly.

3 Each little bird whose song is heard
Through grove and meadow ringing,
At streamlet's brink, will blithely drink,
To tune its voice to singing.

179. Child of the Drunkard.

WM. F. SHERWIN.

Tenderly.

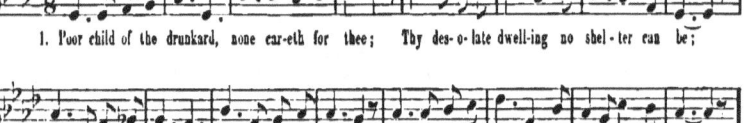

1. Poor child of the drunkard, none car-eth for thee; Thy des-o-late dwell-ing no shel-ter can be;
Friendless and for-sak-en, rude winds on thee blow, Left now to the wide world, say, where canst thou go?
Come hith-er, my dar-ling, Dwell ev-er with me; Here thou shalt be welcome, I'll cheer and comfort thee.

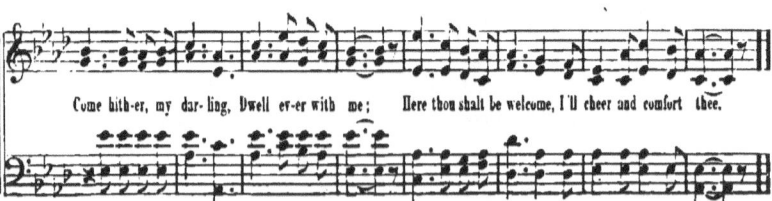

180 The Drunkard's Woe.

W. BENNETT.   W. F. S.

2 Who, in fierce contention striving,
In vain babblings loud engage?
Who from causeless wounds are grieving,
Which no medicine can assuage?

3 Wouldst thou 'scape the drunkard's sorrow?
Wouldst thou shun his dreadful doom?
Wait not for the coming morrow,
Take the pledge, there yet is room.

Child of the Drunkard. Concluded.

2 Low under the green sod thy mother now lies,
Her prayers for thy safety God will not despise;
Her words I remember, oft spoken in faith,
"My child, God will shield thee when I sleep in death."

3 Through years sad and dreary thy dear mother strove
With habits inhuman from him who should love;
Life brought her but sorrow, death brought a rich gain;
Where grief never cometh her spirit doth reign.

4 Thy sad, thoughtless father, how fallen is he!
May God in his mercy the drunkard set free;
Friendless and forsaken, rude winds on thee blow;
Left now to the wide world, say, where canst thou go?

181. Cast Down the Cup.

"At the last it biteth like a serpent, and stingeth like an adder."—PROV. 23:32.

H. TAYLOR.   DR. J. B. HERBERT.

1. There's an ad-der in the cup; There's a woe in ev-'ry sup; Will you dare to drink it up? Cast it down!

CHORUS. Spirited.

Cast it down, cast it down! Now's the day, and now's the hour; Cast it down, cast it down! Then no longer creep and cow'r;
Cast it down, cast it down! Spurn the de-mon and his pow'r; Cast it down, cast it down, cast it down!

2. There's disease in ev'ry glass;
There's remorse and shame, alas!
And a gulf you can not pass;
Cast it down!

3. There is sorrow in the bowl;
There is thirst beyond control;
There is ruin to your soul;
Cast it down!

4. O, then spurn the luring wine!
O, forsake her deadly shrine!
By the help of God divine,
Cast it down!

182. Rally for the Right, Boys.

J. A. B.   J. A. BUTTERFIELD.

1. Like a sol-dier brave, his land to save, Cour-age high and ar-mor bright;
2. For-ward to the fight, strong in the right, Fierce-ly must the bat-tle rage;

Push with vig-or on, and with your might, Now ral-ly for the right, boys, ral-ly!
Vic-t'ry will be ours, if we en-gage To ral-ly for the right, boys, ral-ly!

2 Water, pure water, from heaven distilled,
  Beautiful, beautiful water;
  Drink of the health-giving draught, be filled,
  Nothing is purer or better.
  You who do worship at Bacchus' shrine,
  Thinking to find in it pleasure,
  Leave your potations of deadly wine,
  Drink of the beautiful water.

3 Beautiful water my drink shall be,
  Beautiful, beautiful water;
  Sparkling so bright in its purity,
  Making life joyous forever.
  Strength we will find in the water bright,
  Ne'er the brain will it bewilder;
  Drink as it gleams in the golden light,
  Drink of the beautiful water.

184. "Down in a Dell."

Arranged.

Allegretto.

1. Down in a dell, Near a crystal well, A noble youth was musing; Then he drunk of the stream, And awoke, as from dream, For a bright path, that youth was now choosing.

CHORUS.

"No more wine for me, From custom I'm free as the breeze that plays o'er the mountain, For what drink on earth can afford such pure mirth, As a draught from the crystal fountain?"

2 Far from his home,
 O'er the ocean's foam,
This noble youth was sailing;
 Will he water now choose?
 Will he wine now refuse?
Hark! he sings while his comrades are railing.

3 Bright was the day,
 When a sister gay
Was led to Hymen's altar;
 When our hero was pressed
 To drink wine with a guest;
But he sang, and his voice did not falter.

185. Water is Best.

WM. F. SHERWIN.

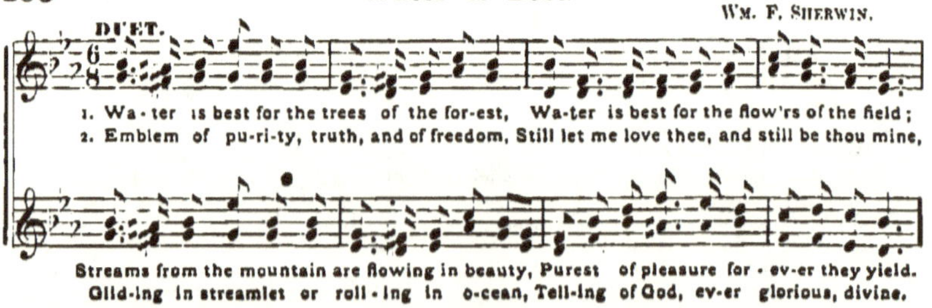

DUET.

1. Water is best for the trees of the forest, Water is best for the flow'rs of the field;
2. Emblem of purity, truth, and of freedom, Still let me love thee, and still be thou mine,

Streams from the mountain are flowing in beauty, Purest of pleasure forever they yield.
Gliding in streamlets or rolling in ocean, Telling of God, ever glorious, divine.

Water is Best. Concluded.

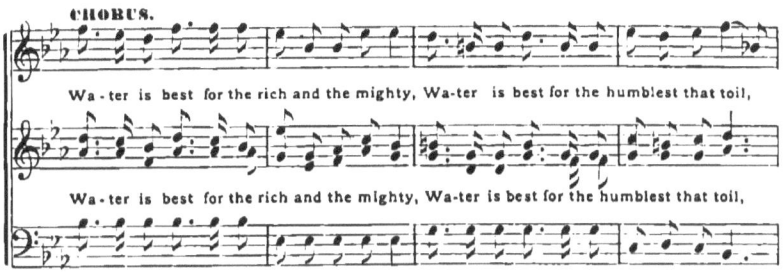

Wa-ter is best for the rich and the mighty, Wa-ter is best for the humblest that toil,

Children and fathers may drink from the fountain, Flowing forever to glad-den the soil.

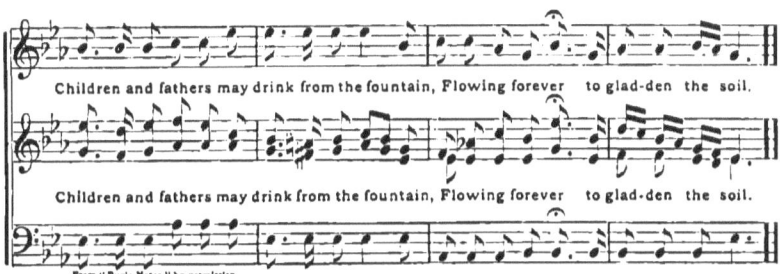

From "Bugle Notes," by permission.

186   Haste to the Rescue.

Arranged.

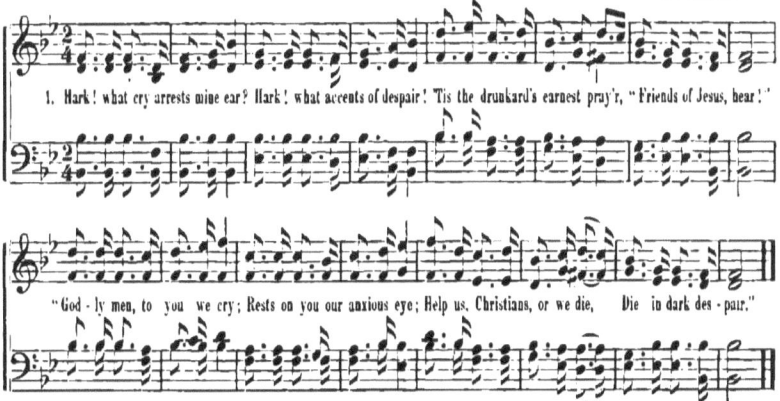

1. Hark! what cry arrests mine ear? Hark! what accents of despair! 'Tis the drunkard's earnest pray'r, "Friends of Jesus, hear!"
"God-ly men, to you we cry; Rests on you our anxious eye; Help us, Christians, or we die, Die in dark des-pair."

2 Hasten, Christians, haste to save
Brothers from the drunkard's grave;
Difficulties boldly brave;
  Hark! for help they call.
Haste, then, to the rescue haste!
See the souls by drink laid waste;
See the work of God defaced,
  In Satan's deadly thrall.

3 Go, then, in the Saviour's name,
Pluck these brands from endless flame,
Deck his royal diadem
  With their ransomed souls.
Work, O, work while yet 'tis day!
Linger not, make no delay;
God will speed you on your way
  To rescue captive souls.

187. Away with the Ruby Wine.

"Look not thou upon the wine when it is red."—PROV. 23: 31.

F. E. BELDEN. W. F. SHERWIN.

1. A-way, a-way with the ru-by wine! We sing in praise of wa-ter! O, give us the crys-tal drink di-vine For ev-'ry son and daugh-ter. From low-ly vale or loft-y moun-tain, Beau-ti-ful and bright it flows, In rip-pling rill and sil-ver fount-ain, As a balm for all our woes.

CHORUS.
A-way, a-way with the ru-by wine! We sing to the praise of wa-ter! A-way, with the nec-tar of the Rhine, And give us the sparkling wa-ter!

2 As fresh and bright as the dew-drops fair,
  The wood and lea adorning;
As free as the bird that knows no care,
  As rosy as the morning,

Is he who quaffs the cup of gladness,
  Held in bounteous nature's hand;
For in its gleam there is no sadness
  For the millions in our land.

188. Angry Words.

"Be ye angry, and sin not."
H. R. PALMER.

1. Angry words! O, let them never From the tongue unbridled slip! May the heart's best impulse ever Check them ere they soil the lip.

CHORUS: "Love one an-oth-er," Thus saith the Sav-iour, Children, obey thy Father's blest command; "Love each other," "Love each other," 'Tis thy Father's blest command; "Love one an-oth-er," Thus saith the Sav-iour, Children, o-bey his blest com-mand. "Love each other," "Love each other," 'Tis his blest com-mand.

2 Love is much too pure and holy;
Friendship is too sacred far,
For a moment's reckless folly
Thus to desolate and mar.

3 Angry words are lightly spoken,
Bitterest thoughts are rashly stirred;
Brightest links of life are broken
By a single angry word.

189. Wise Counsel.

(A hymn six hundred years old.)
C. C. Cline.

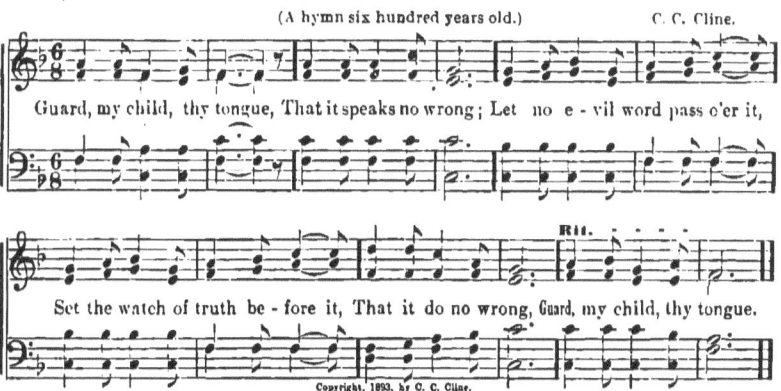

Guard, my child, thy tongue, That it speaks no wrong; Let no e-vil word pass o'er it, Set the watch of truth be-fore it, That it do no wrong, Guard, my child, thy tongue.

Copyright, 1893, by C. C. Cline.

2 Guard, my child, thine eyes;
Prying is not wise;
Let them look on what is right;
From all evil turn their sight;
Prying is not wise,
Guard, my child, thine eyes.

3 Guard, my child, thine ear;
Wicked words will sear;
Let no evil words come in,
That may cause the soul to sin;
Wicked words will sear,
Guard, my child, thine ear.

4 Ear and eye and tongue
Guard while thou art young;
For, alas! these busy three,
Can unruly members be;
Guard while thou art young,
Ears and eyes and tongue.

190. Kind Words are Always Best.

EBEN E. REXFORD.   "A soft answer turneth away wrath."—PROV. 15: 1.   WM. J. KIRKPATRICK.

1. O, speak kind words wher-e'er you be, As thro' this world you go; Let kind-ly deeds be-side your path Like flow'rs of beau-ty grow. The fra-grance of a lov-ing word Will lin-ger in the heart, As sweet-ness haunts the flow'rs we prize When sum-mer days de-part.

CHORUS.
Kind words are al-ways best, Kind words are al-ways best; You will find, where'er you go, Kind words are al-ways best.

Copyright, 1883, by WM. J. KIRKPATRICK.

2 Yes, speak kind words in ev'ry place,
  Although you do not know
The good your loving words may do,
  To those who need them so,
For *God* will know, and surely he,
  In his good time and way,
The giver of a helpful word
  Will royally repay.

3 Then speak kind words, whate'er you do;
  Too brief is human life
To waste the hours as they go by
  In discord and in strife.
Give one and all a loving word—
  Just put them to the test,
And you will find, in ev'ry place,
  Kind words are always best.

191. Speak Gently to the Loving Ones.

MARIA STRAUB.   S. W. STRAUB, by per.

DUET. Tenderly.

1. Speak gently to your father dear, Speak gently to your father, Whose guardian care is over you, Whose earthly fruits you gather.

Speak Gently to the Loving Ones. Concluded.

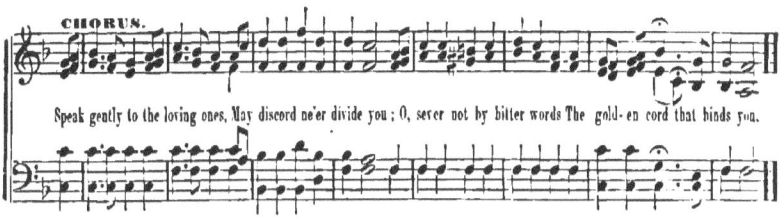

2 Speak gently to your mother dear,
  Speak gently to your mother;
Whose tender love and anxious care,
  Shall ever o'er you hover.

3 Speak gently to your brother dear,
  Speak gently to your brother;

Who would defend your goodly name,
  And shield it from dishonor.

4 Speak gently to your sister dear,
  Speak gently to your sister;
Remember that ofttimes you may
  By kindly words assist her.

192 Kind Words can Never Die.

ABBY HUTCHINSON.

2 Childhood can never die—
  Wrecks of the past
Float o'er the memory,
  Bright to the last.
Many a happy thing,
Many a daisy spring,
Float o'er time's ceaseless wing,
  Far, far away.
Childhood can never die,
  Never die, never die,
Childhood can never die,
  No, never die.

3 Sweet thoughts can never die,
  Though, like the flowers,
Their brightest hues may fly
  In wintry hours.
But when the gentle dew
  Gives them their charms anew,
With many an added hue,
  They bloom again.
Sweet thoughts can never die,
  Never die, never die,
Sweet thoughts can never die,
  No, never die.

4 Our souls can never die,
  Though in the tomb
We may all have to lie,
  Wrapt in its gloom.
What though the flesh decay,
Souls pass in peace away,
Live through eternal day,
  With Christ above.
Our souls can never die,
  Never die, never die,
Our souls can never die,
  No, never die.

193. Scatter Smiles as You Go.

R. S. TAYLOR.   W. B. BRADBURY.

2 Scatter smiles, bright smiles, 't is but little they cost;
But your heart may never know
What a joy they may carry to weary ones
Who are pale with want and woe.

3 Scatter smiles, bright smiles, o'er the grave of the past,
Where the orphan's treasure lies;
In the tear-drop that glistens there light will shine,
As the rainbow paints the skies.

4 Scatter smiles, bright smiles, o'er the young who have strayed
From the path where once they trod;
You may lead to the fountain of truth again,
You may bring them home to God.

5 Scatter smiles, bright smiles, as you pass on your way
Through this world of toil and care;
Like the beams of the morning that gently play,
They will leave a sunlight there.

194. Let it Pass.

Music by R. A. KINZIE.

195 "Tender, and Trusty, and True."

HATTIE TYNG GRISWOLD.   H. S. PERKINS.

1. Let us be tender, and trusty, and true—Here is a tho't, dearest children, for you;
Where'er we go, and what-ev-er we do, Let us be tender, and trusty, and true.

CHORUS. Earnest.

Brave to the battle of life we will go, Tender and trusty in all that we do;
Helpful and thoughtful to all we will prove, Winning all hearts by our goodness and love.

2 Let us be trusty, and tender and true—
Children, I pray you to keep this in view;
Blessing each other, our blessing we find,
Therefore be helpful, and tho'tful, and kind.

3 Let us be cheerful and happy as well,
That all our life-service doubly may tell;
God loves the cheerful heart singing its lay,
Let us then joyously keep on our way.

Let it Pass. Concluded.

2 Echo not an angry word;
   Let it pass, let it pass!
Think how often you have erred;
   Let it pass, let it pass!
Since our joys must pass away,
Like the dew-drops on the way,
Wherefore should our sorrows stay?
   Let them pass, let them pass!

3 If for good you've taken ill,
   Let it pass, let it pass!
O! be kind and gentle still;
   Let it pass, let it pass!
Time at last makes all things straight;
Let us not resent, but wait,
And our triumph shall be great;
   Let it pass, let it pass!

196. Honor Bright.

W. A. O. W. A. O.

1. Hon-or bright, hon-or bright! Try to keep your honor bright; Do not soil it with a lie, In-to secrets do not pry, But with heart and soul, O, try To keep your honor bright.

CHORUS. Bis.

{ Saying, "God helping me!" }
{ Praying, "God helping me!" } Trusting not a-lone in self To keep your honor bright.

From "Way of Life," by permission of W. W. Whitney.

2 Honor bright, honor bright!
Try to keep your honor bright;
Do not break the Sabbath day,
Be not angry in your play,
But with resolution say,
"I'll keep my honor bright."

3 Honor bright, honor bright!
Try to keep your honor bright;
Take not God's dear name in vain,
Nor of what he sends complain,
But resolve, with might and main,
To keep your honor bright.

197. What Makes Us Happy?

Sprightly. D. C.

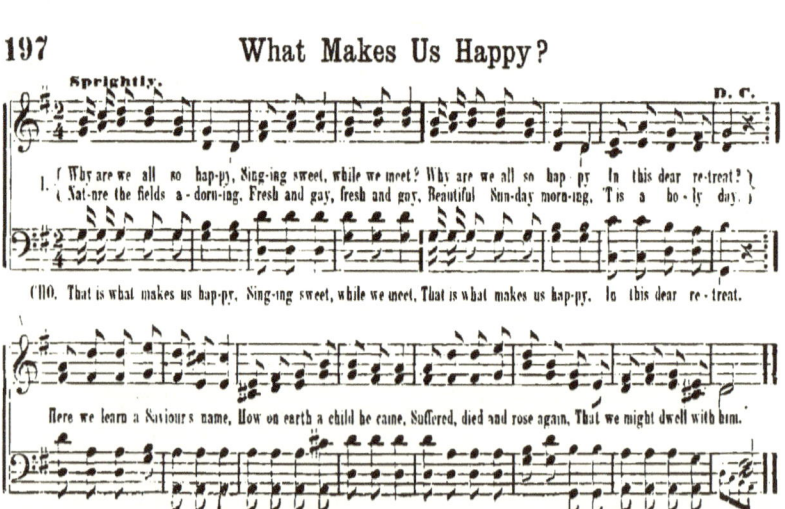

1. { Why are we all so hap-py, Sing-ing sweet, while we meet? Why are we all so hap-py In this dear re-treat? }
   { Nat-ure the fields a-dorn-ing, Fresh and gay, fresh and gay, Beautiful Sun-day morn-ing, 'T is a ho-ly day. }

CHO. That is what makes us hap-py, Sing-ing sweet, while we meet, That is what makes us hap-py, In this dear re-treat.

Here we learn a Saviour's name, How on earth a child he came, Suffered, died and rose again, That we might dwell with him.

198. Rifted Clouds.

MARY COLBY. "Joyful in tribulation." T. C. O'KANE.

1. There is rarely a day so sunny But a little cloud appears; There is never a life so happy But has had its time of tears; Yet the sun shines out the brighter When the stormy tempest clears.

CHORUS.
In the sunshine or the shade, Let us ever cheerful be, Ever trusting in our Saviour's boundless grace, boundless grace; Soon will shadows pass away, Thro' the rifted clouds we'll see The Redeemer's smiling face.

2 There is rarely a cup so pleasant
But has bitter with the sweet;
There is never a path so rugged,
Bearing not the print of feet,
But we have a Helper furnished
For the trials we may meet.

3 There is never a way so narrow
But the entrance is made straight;
There is always a hand to help us
To approach the upper gate,
For the angels will be nearest
To a soul that's desolate.

4 There is never a heart so haughty
But will some day bow and kneel;
There is never a heart so wounded
That the Saviour can not heal;
There is many a lowly forehead
Bearing now the hidden seal.

What Makes Us Happy? Concluded.

2 What are the wild birds singing?
Full of glee, full of glee,
Swiftly their pinions winging
O'er the flowery lea,
Praising the God who made them,
Free as air—free as air,
Kindly his hand arrayed them
In the plumes they wear.
Wood and stream and meadow gay,
Join the merry, merry lay;
All are praising God to-day,
And we will praise him too.

3 What are the angels singing?
Robed in white, crowned with light,
Ever their music ringing,
In that world so bright,
Singing of grace and glory,
Sweet and clear —sweet and clear,
Telling the wondrous story
Children love so dear.
Happy, happy angel band,
Round our Father's throne they stand
In that pure and sunny land,
Our home beyond the sky.

199. Let Us Arise.

E. D. Mund.
E. S. Lorenz.

1. Do you slumber in your tent, Christian Soldier, While the foe is spreading woe through the land? Do you note his rising pow'r, Growing bolder ev'ry hour? Will he not our land devour, while you stand?

D. S.—Though our numbers may be few, God will lead us grandly thro', And our arms with strength endue by his might.

CHORUS.

Let us arise! all unite! Let us arise! in our might! Let us arise! speak for God and the right.

Used by permission of E. S. Lorenz, owner of the Copyright.

2 Can you sleep while homes are rent, Christian Soldier?
Are not heavens turned to hells by his power?
Mark you not the mother's sigh?
Hear you not the children's cry?
See you not their loved ones die, every hour?

3 Can you linger in your tent, Christian Soldier?
Satan's smiling o'er your idle delay;
Thousands perish while you wait,
While you counsel and debate;
Heed you not their awful fate, as they stray?

4 Let us rise in holy wrath, Christian Soldiers,
Crush the evil 'neath the heel of our might!
Counting cost, no longer wait,
Forward, manhood of the state,
For in God our strength is great for the right.

200. Only a Penny Apiece.

Paulina.
O. Blackman.

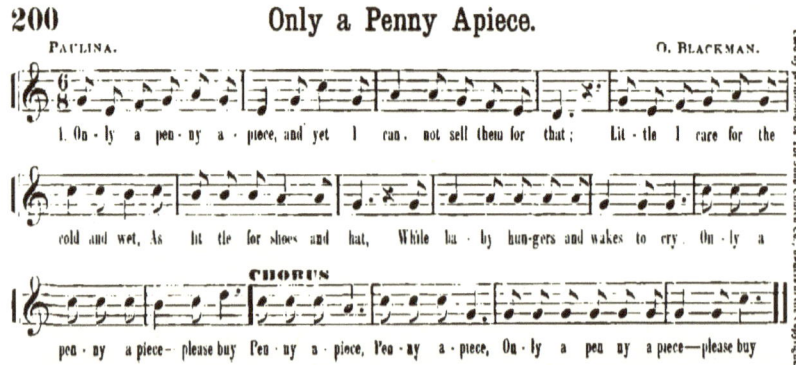

1. Only a penny apiece, and yet I cannot sell them for that; Little I care for the cold and wet, As little for shoes and hat, While baby hungers and wakes to cry. Only a penny apiece—please buy Penny apiece, Penny apiece, Only a penny apiece—please buy

Used by permission of The John Church Co., owners of the Copyright.

201. Be Kind to the Loved Ones at Home.

I. B. WOODBURY.

1. Be kind to thy father, for when thou wert young, Who loved thee so fondly as he? He caught the first accents that fell from thy tongue, And joined in thy in-no-cent glee. Be kind to thy fa-ther, for now he is old, His locks in-ter-mingled with gray; His footsteps are feeble, once fear-less and bold, Thy fa-ther is pass-ing a-way.

2 Be kind to thy mother, for lo! on her brow
  May traces of sorrow be seen;
O well may'st thou cherish and comfort her now,
  For loving and kind hath she been.
Remember thy mother, for thee will she pray,
  As long as God giveth her breath;
With accents of kindness then cheer her lone way,
  E'en to the dark valley of death.

3 Be kind to thy brother—his heart will have dearth,
  If the smile of thy joy be withdrawn;
The flowers of feeling will fail at their birth,
  If the dew of affection be gone.
Be kind to thy brother—wherever you are,
  The love of a brother shall be
An ornament purer and richer by far
  Than pearls from the depth of the sea.

4 Be kind to thy sister—not many may know
  The depth of true sisterly love;
The wealth of the ocean lies fathoms below
  The surface that sparkles above.
Be kind to thy father, once fearless and bold,
  Be kind to thy mother so near;
Be kind to thy brother, nor show thy heart cold,
  Be kind to thy sister so dear.

Only a Penny Apiece. Concluded.

2 Many a mile have I walked to-day,
  My feet are weary and sore;
Many a tear have I wept away,
  But now I must weep no more;
The stars look down with their searching eye,
Only a penny apiece—please buy.

3 O, for a home in the better land,
  In place of yon wretched cot;
O, for a loaf for the thin, blue hand,
  That would clutch what I have not;
They watch for me with an eager eye,
Only a penny apiece—please buy.

202. Love at Home.

J. H. McNaughton.

1. There is beau-ty all a-round, When there's love at home; There is joy in ev-'ry sound, When there's love at home. Peace and plen-ty here a-bide, Smil-ing sweet on ev-'ry side, Time doth soft-ly, sweet-ly glide, When there's love at home. Love at home, love at home; Time doth softly, sweetly glide, When there's love at home.

2 In the cottage there is joy,
When there's love at home;
Hate and envy ne'er annoy,
When there's love at home.
Roses blossom 'neath our feet,
All the earth's a garden sweet,
Making life a bliss complete,
When there's love at home.

3 Kindly heaven smiles above,
When there's love at home;
All the earth is filled with love,
When there's love at home.
Sweeter sings the brooklet by,
Brighter beams the azure sky;
O, there's One who smiles on high,
When there's love at home.

4 Jesus, show thy mercy mine,
Then there's love at home;
Sweetly whisper, I am thine;
Then there's love at home.
Source of love, thy cheering light
Far exceeds the sun so bright—
Can dispel the gloom of night;
Then there's love at home.

203. The Sparkling Rill.

James B. Taylor.

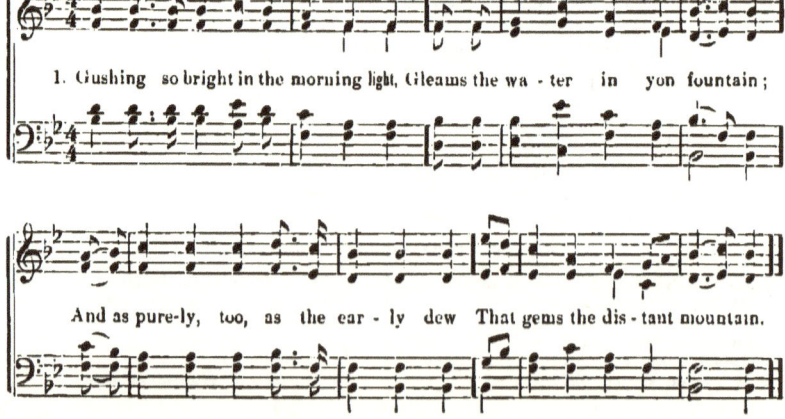

1. Gushing so bright in the morning light, Gleams the wa-ter in yon fountain; And as pure-ly, too, as the ear-ly dew That gems the dis-tant mountain.

The Sparkling Rill. Concluded.

2 Quietly glide in their silvery tide,
  Pearly brooks from rocks to valley;
And the dashing streams in the strong sun-
  Like bannered armies rally.   [beams
3 Touch not the wine, though it brightly shine,
  When a purer draught is given:

A gift so sweet, all our wants to meet,
  A beverage bright from heaven.
4 O fountain clear, with a heart sincere
  We will praise thy glorious Giver;
And when we rise to our native skies,
  We'll drink of life's bright river.

204 Help a Little.

"By love serve one another."—GAL 5: 13.

MRS. E. C. ELLSWORTH.   WM. J. KIRKPATRICK.

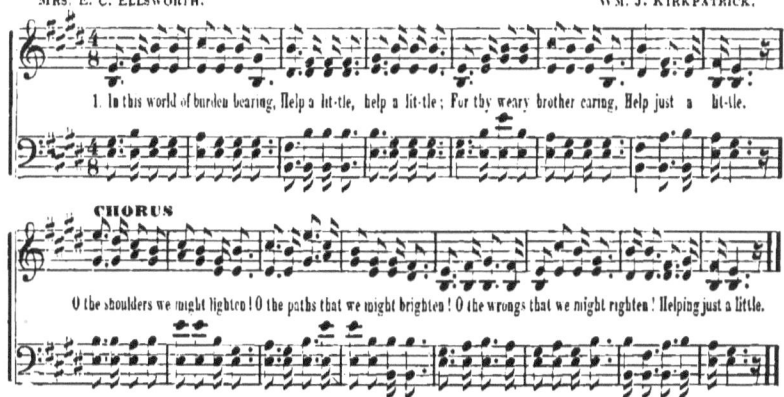

2 In the work around us pressing,
    Help a little, help a little;
  Let thy labor prove a blessing,
    Help just a little.
3 In the seed-time's early sowing,
    Help a little, help a little;

On the soil some care bestowing,
    Help just a little.
4 When the reapers sheaves are binding,
    Help a little, help a little;
  O some handfuls then be finding,
    Help just a little.

205. Have You Counted the Cost, My Boy?

MRS. C. L. SHACKLOCK.　　　　　　　　　　　J. M. STILLMAN.

1. There's an am-ber line in the sparkling draught, And it brings to your eyes the light; And your heart beats high when the bowl is quaffed: Do you think of its cost to-night? It will cost you wealth, it will cost you health, It will rob you of peace and joy: Will you drink, will you drink at so great a price? Will you drink, will you drink, my boy?

Copyright, 1883, by H. L. Basham & Co.

2 Not the silver coin, but the wasted years,
With their promise so true and bright;
And the cup is bought with a mother's tears:
Will you drink, will you drink to-night?

3 It bears on its foam the wreck of your home,
Of your life with its honor lost;
'Tis filled with remorse for the days to come:
Can you drink at so great a cost?

206. Help the Drinking Man.

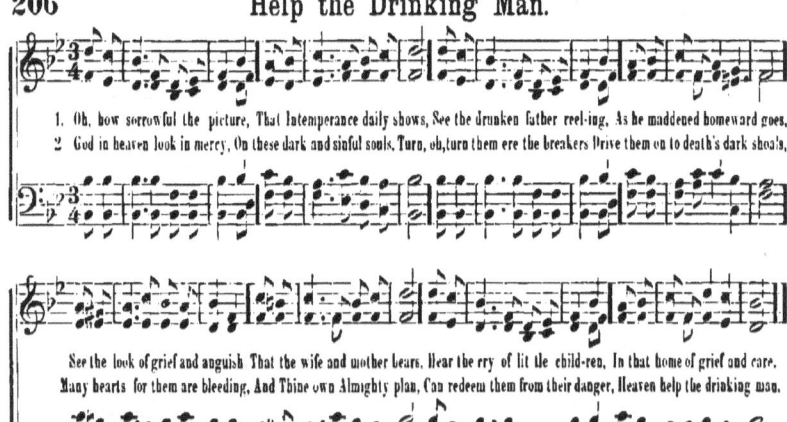

1. Oh, how sorrowful the picture, That Intemperance daily shows, See the drunken father reel-ing, As he maddened homeward goes, See the look of grief and anguish That the wife and mother bears, Hear the cry of lit tle child-ren, In that home of grief and care.

2 God in heaven look in mercy, On these dark and sinful souls, Turn, oh, turn them ere the breakers Drive them on to death's dark shoals, Many hearts for them are bleeding, And Thine own Almighty plan, Can redeem them from their danger, Heaven help the drinking man.

Help the Drinking Man. Concluded.

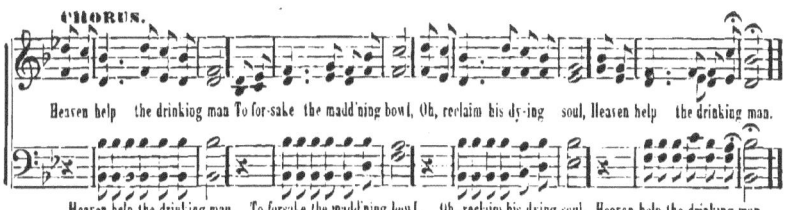

CHORUS.
Heaven help the drinking man To for-sake the madd'ning bowl, Oh, reclaim his dy-ing soul, Heaven help the drinking man.
Heaven help the drinking man To forsake the madd'ning bowl, Oh, reclaim his dying soul, Heaven help the drinking man.

207 Touch Not the Cup.

JAMES H. AIKMAN. T. H. BAYLY.

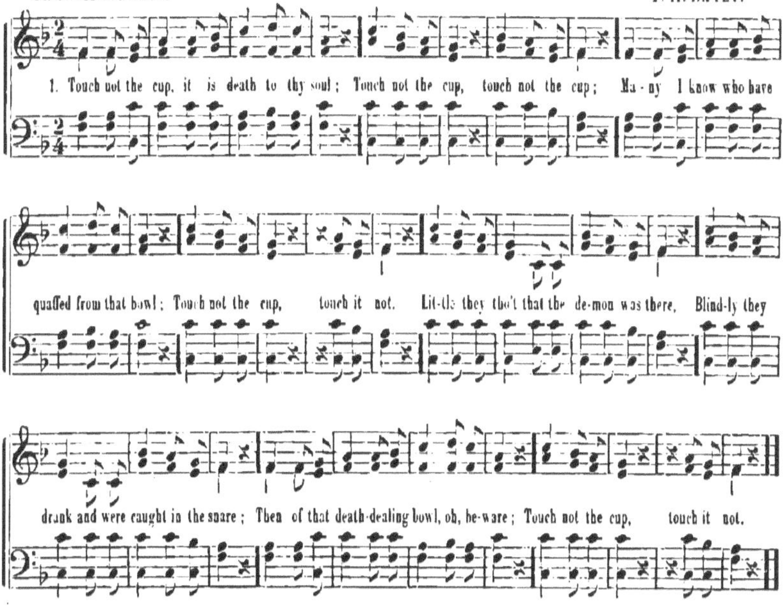
1. Touch not the cup, it is death to thy soul; Touch not the cup, touch not the cup; Ma-ny I know who have
quaffed from that bowl; Touch not the cup, touch it not. Lit-tle they tho't that the de-mon was there, Blind-ly they
drank and were caught in the snare; Then of that death-dealing bowl, oh, be-ware; Touch not the cup, touch it not.

2 Touch not the cup when the wine glistens bright;
Though like the ruby it shines in the light;
Fangs of the serpent are hid in the bowl,
Deeply the poison may enter thy soul,
Soon will it plunge thee beyond thy control.

3 Touch not the cup, young man in thy pride;
Hark to the warning of thousands who've died;
Go to their lonely and desolate tomb,
Think of their death, of their sorrow and gloom;
Think that perhaps thou may'st share in their doom.

4 Touch not the cup, oh, drink not a drop;
All that thou lovest entreat thee to stop;
Stop! for the home that to thee is so dear,
Stop! for the friends that to thee are so near,
Stop! for thy country, in trembling and fear.

208. Don't Forget the Old Folks.

L. S. LEASON, by per.

1. Don't for-get the old folks, Love them more and more; As they turn their longing eyes T'ward the golden shore.

Let your words be ten-der, Loving, soft, and low; Let their last days be the best They have known below,

CHORUS.

Don't forget the old folks, Life will soon be o'er; Guide them till their weary feet Tread the golden shore.

2 Don't forget poor father,
   With his failing sight;
  With his locks once thick and brown,
   Scanty now and white;
  Tho' he may be childish,
   Still do you be kind;
  Think of him as years ago,
   With his master mind.

3 Don't forget dear mother,
   With her furrowed brow;
  All the light of other years,
   Time has faded now;
  Memory is waning,
   Soon its light will fail;
  Guide her gently, till she stands
   Safe within the vale.

209. Touch Not.

MRS. M. B. C. SLADE.   R. M. McINTOSH, by per.

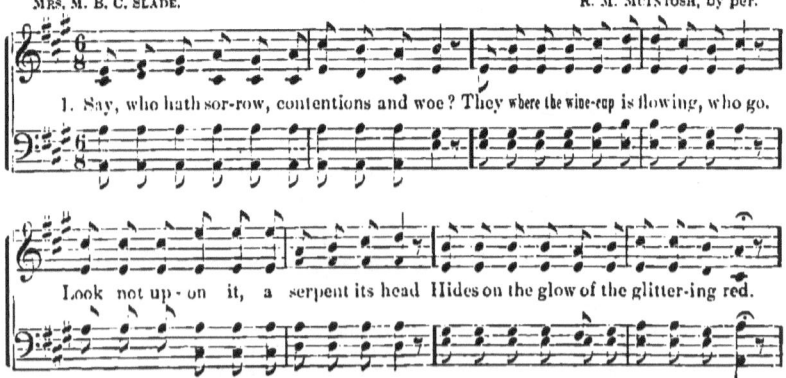

1. Say, who hath sor-row, contentions and woe? They where the wine-cup is flowing, who go.

Look not up-on it, a serpent its head Hides on the glow of the glitter-ing red.

Touch Not. Concluded.

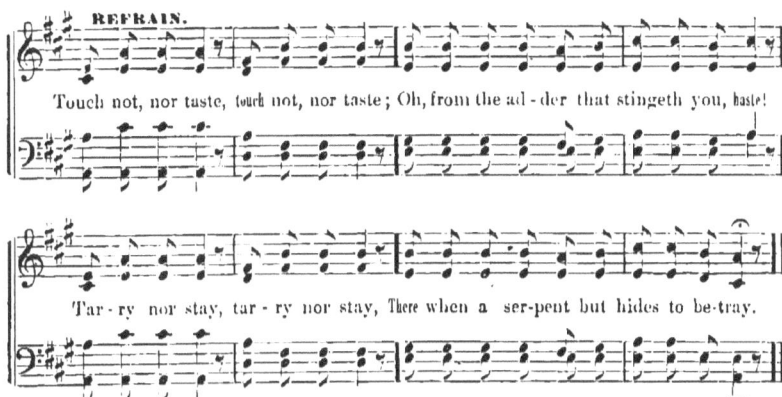

2 Say, who in spirit are wounded, in pain?
They who go seeking the wine-cup again;
Tarrying long till the sparkle is past,
Lo, it shall sting like an adder at last.

3 Say, who is stricken until he must be
Like as one toss'd in the midst of the sea?

They who are beaten and sickened and sore,
They who have fallen the wine-cup before.

4 What shall we tell them, oh, what can we say?
How can we turn them from sinning away?
Lovingly give them the brotherly hand,
Tenderly helping the fallen to stand.

210   The Steeds of Sin.

W. O. BEMIS.   W. A. LAFFERTY.

2 Intemperance with gory eyes,
  Goes speeding o'er the earth;
A death in all his pathway lies,
  He's of a fiendish birth.
Ride not this fleet and foaming steed,
  The vict'ry he shall win;
What rein or bit can stay his speed,
  To doom of deadly sin.

3 Oh, there are other dreadful steeds,
  That man oft dares to ride;
That work upon the beauteous earth,
  Invasion dark and wide.
Ride not the steeds of sin, my boy,
  Of their swift hoofs beware;
They have a hot consuming breath,
  And poisoned with despair.

211. Right Men are Wanted.

1. Right men are wanted high places to fill, Men of good manners, of wisdom and skill; Drunkards can never attain to the prize. We must be abstainers, for we all want to rise.
2. Drunkards begin with a small glass or so, None are secure but abstainers, we know; Health, time and money are talents we prize, We must be abstainers, for we all want to rise.

CHORUS.
Break the pledge, never, no, no, no! Not while the stream in the valleys shall flow, Dear are the treasures which temp'rance can tell, Health and pleasure follow when we drink from the well.

212. The Wine Cup.

MRS. FANNY CROSBY.   S. C. FOSTER.

1. O! be warned of your danger, nor slight the day of grace, The wine cup leads to sin and woe;
'Tis the Saviour that calls you, O fly to his embrace, What joy his mercy can bestow!
D.C. For the world and its pleasures are fleeting as a dream, O come, and be forever blest.

CHORUS.
See the fount of salvation before you, Drink, O drink, and find a peaceful rest;

2 Shall your homes still be lonely, and pity strive in vain,
To wake one feeling in your heart?
Will you doom those who love you to sorrow, grief and pain?
O, come, and choose the better part.

3 Break the chain that would bind you, that sparkles to deceive,
Be warned while yet you may return;
If the spirit now striving too often you should grieve,
The lamp of life may cease to burn.

214. Save the Boy.

L. F. C. L. F. COLE.

1 Once he sat upon my knee,
  Look'd from sweet eyes into mine,
  Questioned me so wondrously
  Of the mysteries divine;
  Once he fondly clasped my neck,
  Pressed my cheek with kisses sweet;
  Oh, my heart, we little reck
  Where may roam the precious feet.

2 Once his laugh with merry ring
  Filled our house with music rare,
  And his loving hands would bring
  Wreaths of blossoms for my hair;
  Oh, the merry, happy sprite,
  Constant, ceaseless source of joy;
  But to-night, O God, to-night,
  Where, oh, where's my wand'ring boy?

3 Midst the glitter and the glare
  Of the room where death is dealt,
  Scarce you'd know him, but he's there,
  He who once so rev'rent knelt
  At my knee, and softly spoke
  Words into the ear of God;
  Oh, my heart, 'tis smitten, broke,
  Crushed, I bend beneath the rod.

4 Oh, this curse has spoiled my boy!
  Led him down and down to death;
  Robbed me of my rarest joy,
  Made a pang of ev'ry breath;
  Mothers, fathers, hear my plea!
  Let your pleadings pierce the sky,
  Pray and work most earnestly,
  Let us save our boys or die.

By per. of Messrs. Towne & Stillman, owners of copyright.

215. Love is Kind.

Rev. Henry Burton.   Wm. J. Kirkpatrick. By per.

Copyright, 1868, by W. J. Kirkpatrick.

2 Did you hear the loving word?
    Send it forth,
Like the singing of a bird?
    Send it forth! send it forth!
Let its music live and grow,
Let it cheer another's woe;
You have reaped what others sow,
    Send it forth! send it forth!

3 Have you found the heavenly light?
    Let it shine,
Souls are groping in the night,
    Let it shine, let it shine!
Hold your lighted lamp on high,
Be a star in some one's sky,
He may live who else would die,
    Let it shine, let it shine.

NATURE'S MELODIES.

The heavens declare the glory of God and the firmament showeth his handiwork.—Ps. 19 : 1.

220   Welcome to Morning.

M. B. C. SLADE.   OFFENBACH.

The sun is ris-ing o'er the o-cean, The smil-ing wa-ters greet the day,
And joy-ous winds to danc-ing mo-tion, Wake the bil-lows of the day.

TRIO.

See, where the clouds roll up the mountains; Night has her mist-y ban-ner furled;
And spring-ing from a thou-sand fountains, Light and joy o'er-flow the world.

Welcome to Morning. Concluded.

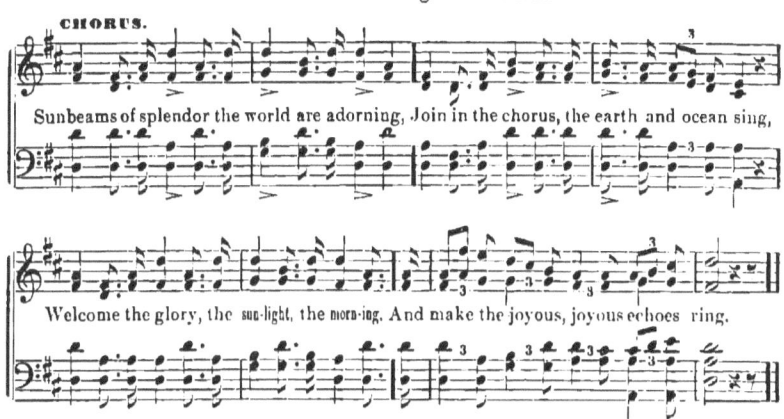

Sunbeams of splendor the world are adorning, Join in the chorus, the earth and ocean sing, Welcome the glory, the sun-light, the morn-ing. And make the joyous, joyous echoes ring.

2 The birds flit o'er the dewy meadows;
 They carol sweet in branches high:
While down the vales the frightened shadows
 Hasten from the dawn to day.
Rocked on the water's placid bosom,
 Purely the water lilies gleam,
While willow branch and bending blossom,
 Bid good morrow to the stream.

3 Oh, come, let clouds of grief and sadness,
 Fly swift as shades of night away;
Let all our hearts, like birds of gladness,
 Welcome in the glad new day.
Bright flow'rs, and streams, and birds of heaven,
 Incense and praises waft above;
From hearts and voices now be given,
 Songs of praise, and joy, and love.

221 Twilight is Falling.

A. S. Keiffer. B. C. Unseld.

1. Twilight is stealing O-ver the sea; Shadows are falling Dark on the lea; Borne on the night winds,

For Cho. Gleameth a mansion

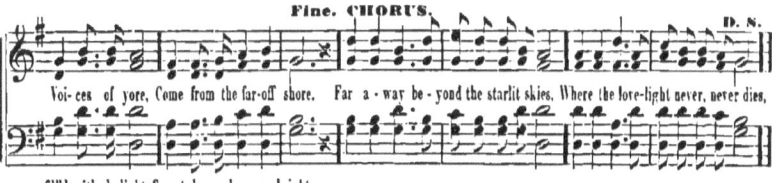

Voi-ces of yore, Come from the far-off shore. Far a-way be-yond the starlit skies, Where the love-light never, never dies,

fill'd with de-light, Sweet, happy home so bright.

2 Voices of lov'd ones! songs of the past!
Still linger round me, while life shall last;
Lonely I wander, sadly I roam,
Seeking that far-off home.

3 Come in the twilight, come, come to me!
Bringing some message over the sea,
Cheering my pathway, while here I roam,
Seeking that far-off home.

222 'Tis Summer Time.

W. A. OGDEN.

Copyright, 1891, by Robert L. Fletcher.

2 The sun is brightly beaming,
    All nature smiles to-day;
   The golden light is gleaming
    To cheer the onward way;
   In holy contemplation
    We look to God above;
   We praise him for salvation,
    And all his wondrous love.

3 This day of floral greeting,
    We come a happy throng,
   And spend the moments fleeting,
    In mirth and joyful song;
   Oh, day of richest treasure!
    Oh, day among the flowers!
   We sing in tuneful measure,
    To bless the waking hours.

223 Buds of Promise.

MRS. JOS. F. KNAPP.

224. O What Can You Tell.

ROSSITER W. RAYMOND. J. C. LOWRY, 1880.

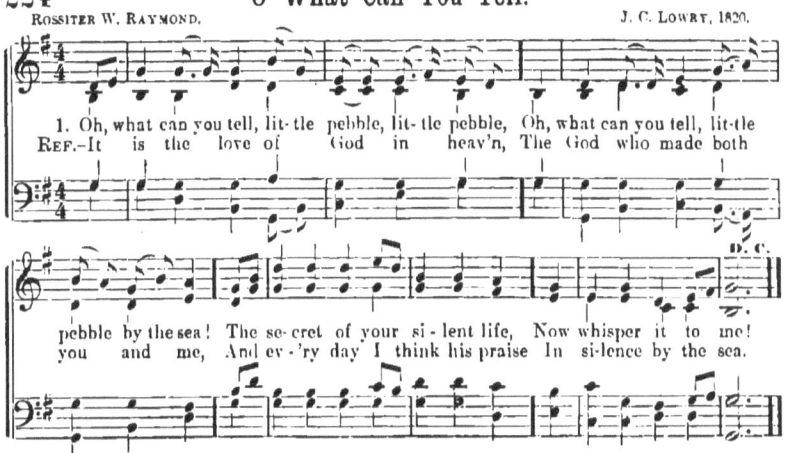

1. Oh, what can you tell, lit-tle pebble, lit-tle pebble, Oh, what can you tell, lit-tle pebble by the sea! The se-cret of your si-lent life, Now whisper it to me!

REF.—It is the love of God in heav'n, The God who made both you and me, And ev-'ry day I think his praise In si-lence by the sea.

2 Oh, what can you tell, little flower, little flower,
Oh, what can you tell, little flower on the lea?
The secret of your sweet perfume,
Now whisper it to me!
REF.—It is the love of God in heav'n,
The God who made both you and me,
And every day I breathe his praise
In fragrance on the lea.

3 Oh, what can you tell, little bird, little bird.
Oh, what can you tell, little bird upon the tree!
The secret of your joyous song,
Now whisper it to me!
REF.—It is the love of God in heav'n,
The God who made both you and me,

And every day I sing his praise
Upon the summer tree.

4 Oh, what can you tell, little child, little child.
Oh, what can you tell, little child upon my knee!
The secret of your happy smile,
Now whisper it to me!
REF.—It is the love of God in heav'n,
The God who made both you and me,
And every day I seek his praise
Upon my bended knee!

FULL CHO.—Thus to the love of God in heav'n,
The God who made both you and me,
The praise of all things here is giv'n!
And evermore shall be!

Buds of Promise. Concluded.

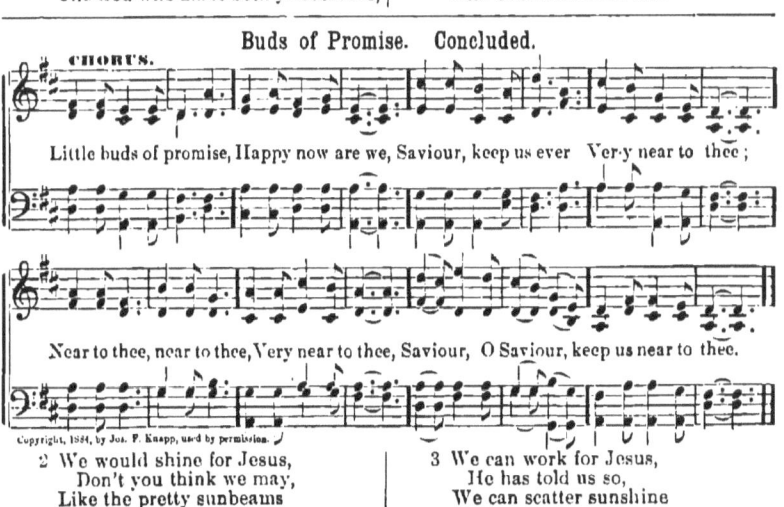

CHORUS.

Little buds of promise, Happy now are we, Saviour, keep us ever Ver-y near to thee;
Near to thee, near to thee, Very near to thee, Saviour, O Saviour, keep us near to thee.

Copyright, 1884, by Jos. F. Knapp, used by permission.

2 We would shine for Jesus,
Don't you think we may,
Like the pretty sunbeams
Shining on our way.

3 We can work for Jesus,
He has told us so,
We can scatter sunshine
Every-where we go.

225. Wake the Morning.

Arr. by W. B. Hall.

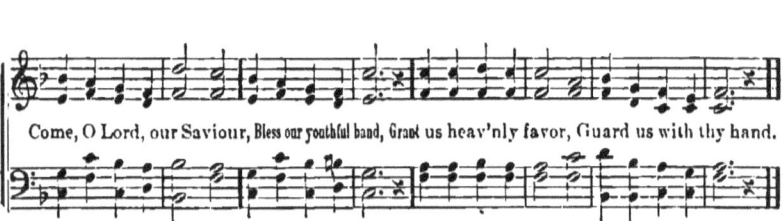

Wake, wake the morning; Bright the golden ray, All our hearts rejoicing, Hail the new-born day;
Come, O Lord, our Saviour, Bless our youthful band, Grant us heav'nly favor, Guard us with thy hand.

2 Wake, wake the morning;
Happy, happy day;
All our hearts and voices
Grateful homage pay.
May the King of Glory,
From his throne above,
Shed his gentle spirit,
Fill our hearts with love.

3 Wake, wake the morning;
Joyful tidings bear;
Children's hearts and voices
Blend in grateful pray'r.
Come, O Lord, our Saviour,
Make us all thine own,
Like the pure, sweet angels,
Dwelling round thy throne.

226. Catch the Sunshine.

Allegretto.

1. Catch the sunshine! tho' it flickers Thro' a dark and dismal cloud; Tho' it falls so faint and fee-ble On a heart with sorrow bow'd;
Catch it quickly! it is passing, Passing rap-id-ly a-way; It has on-ly come to tell you There is yet a brighter day.

2 Catch the sunshine! tho' life's tempest
May unfurl its chilling blast;
Catch the little hopeful stranger!
Storms will not forever last.
Don't give up and say, Forsaken!
Don't begin to say, I'm sad!
Look! there comes a gleam of sunshine!
Catch it! it will make you glad!

3 Catch the sunshine! don't be grieving;
O'er thy sorrows ne'er despair;
Life's a sea of stormy billows—
We must meet them everywhere;
Pass right through them! do not tarry;
Overcome the heaving tide;
There's a sparkling gleam of sunshine
Waiting on the other side.

227. Beautiful Things.

JAMES H. CROXALL.

2 Beautiful sun that shines so bright,
Beautiful stars with glittering light,
Beautiful summer, beautiful spring,
Beautiful birds that merrily sing.

3 Beautiful lambs, that frisk and play,
Beautiful night and beautiful day,

Beautiful lily, beautiful rose,
Beautiful ev'ry flow'r that grows.

4 Beautiful drops of pearly dew,
Beautiful hills and vales to view,
Beautiful herbs that scent the air,
Beautiful things grow ev'rywhere.

228. See the Snow Come Down.

J. R. M.   "Wash me, and I shall be whiter than snow."—Ps. 51: 7.   J. R. M.

Used by permission of The John Church Co., owners of the Copyright.

2 See the snow come down,
See the snow come down!
Ah! we have need of its spotless white,
Need of the lesson it brings to all;
Ah! we have need that its mantle bright
Shall over our poor hearts fall.

3 See the snow come down,
See the snow come down!
Think of the Father who loveth still,
Giving us promise where'er we go,
That some day, somewhere, in his good will,
Our hearts shall be white as snow.

229. Why Do the Lovely Flowers Bloom?

S. W. STRAUB.　　　　　　　S. W. STRAUB, by per.

2 Why do the lovely flowers bloom?
By palace or by cottage wall,
For high or low, for rich or poor,
Alike they bloom, they bloom for all.

3 Why do the lovely flowers bloom?
Why smile thus on our path alway?
Through valley or on mountain side,
They cheer us onward day by day.

230. Pleasant Weather.

Pleasant Weather. Concluded.

plain, Thank him, for the gold-en sun - shine, And the sil-ver rain, And the sil-ver rain, And the sil-ver rain.

2 Thank God of good the Giver!
Shout it, sportive little breeze;
Respond, O tuneful river,
To the nodding little trees.
Thank him, thank him, bird and birdling,
Thank him as ye grow and sing;
Thank him, mingle in thanksgiving,
Every living thing.

3 Thank God with cheerful spirit,
In a glow of present love,
For what we here inherit,
And our blessed hopes above.
Thank him; Universal Nature
Revels in her birth,
When God, in pleasant weather,
Smiles upon the earth.

231 Winter is Coming.

S. E. SIMPSON ELY. By per.

The winter is coming, is coming, The snowflakes beginning to fall; White messengers sent from the north winds, Bring sorrow or gladness to all. The snow birds in dooryards are chirp-ing, Sweet angels of winter they come; And bluebirds and redbreasted rob - ins To far away Southlands have flown.

From Loving Voices.

2 The last rose of summer is fading,
Petunias and dahlias are gone;
The green-tufted garments of summer,
Give place to the snowy white gown.
The trees have cast off their green dresses,
Old earth is now shivering and bare;
And everywhere read we the lesson,
For Winter's fierce blasts now prepare.

3 The winter of life, too, is coming,
Is coming to you and to me;
When the vigor and action of childhood,
Our portion will nevermore be.
Then work, for life's winter is coming,
Oh, lay up your treasure in store,
In Jesus' own heavenly garner,
Where winters are feared nevermore.

232. Song of the Lilies.

J. A. COLLIER. "Consider the lilies of the field." W. B. BRADBURY.

1. Hark, the lil-ies whis-per Ten-der-ly and low, "In our grace and beau-ty See how fair we grow," Thus our heav'n-ly Fa-ther Cares for all be-low. The lil-ies of the field, The beau-ti-ful lil-ies of the field, Your Fa-ther cares for them, And shall he not care for you?

Used by permission of The Biglow & Main Co., owners of the Copyright.

2 Hark, the roses speaking,
Telling all abroad
Their sweet wondrous story
Of the love of God,
In the Rose of Sharon,
Jesus Christ, the Lord.
The roses, how they bloom!
The beautiful roses, how they bloom!
Your Father cares for them,
And shall he not care for you?

3 Let us, then, be trustful,
Doubting not, although
Much of toil and trouble
Be our lot below.
Think upon the lilies,
See how fair they grow;
The lilies of the field,
The beautiful lilies of the field;
Your Father cares for them,
And shall he not care for you?

233. God is Ever Good.

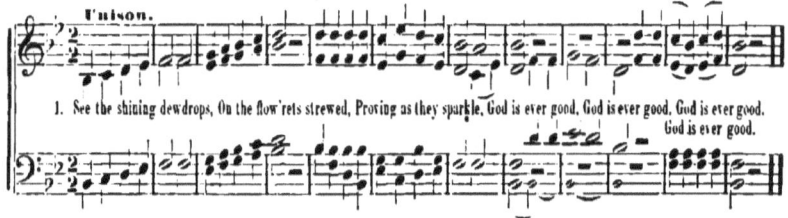

1. See the shining dewdrops, On the flow'rets strewed, Proving as they sparkle, God is ever good, God is ever good, God is ever good. God is ever good.

2 See the morning sunbeams
Lighting up the wood,
Silently proclaiming—
God is ever good, etc.

3 Hear the mountain streamlet,
In the solitude,
With its ripple saying,
God is ever good, etc.

4 In the leafy treetops,
Where no fears intrude,
Joyous birds are singing,
God is ever good, etc.

5 Bring, my heart, thy tribute,
Songs of gratitude,
While all nature utters,
God is ever good, etc.

HOME AND HEAVEN.

"In my Father's house are many mansions, if it were not so I would have told you."—Jno. 14: 2.

240 Walking the Golden Streets.

A. S. Doughty. Geo. C. Hugg.

1. Who, who are these clothed in garments pure and white, Walking the streets of that cit-y fair and bright. Dwelling in light where no burn-ing rays are known, Standing near the great e-ter-nal throne.

CHORUS.
Walk . . . ing thro' the streets, . . . Walk . . . ing thro' the streets, . . .
Walking thro' the streets, thro' the beautiful golden streets, Walking thro' the streets, thro' the beautiful golden streets,
Walk . . . ing through the streets, . . . Of the New Je-ru-sa-lem.
Walk-ing through the streets, through the beau-ti-ful gold-en streets,

Copyright, 1889, by Hugg & Armstrong, used by permission.

2 These, these are they who through tribulation came,
Bearing the cross—who endured reproach and shame;
Having their robes washed in blood of Calvary's Lamb,
Therefore do they bear the conqueror's palm.

3 Therefore they dwell with the Saviour they behold,
Walk through the streets that are paved with purest gold;
Freed from all sorrow, they shout o'er conflict past,
Praise to Jesus—victory at last!

241. The Crystal Stream.

Unknown.   Amos 5: 8.   T. W. Hubbard.

1. Over the river the crystal stream flows, Over the river the tree of life grows, Over the river each lone pilgrim goes, Thro' the dim portals of death. Close by our threshold the dark angel stands, Beck'ning us on with his pale, trembling hands; Chilling our hearts with the cold, icy hands, Stealing each quivering breath.

CHORUS. Over the river, Over the river, Over the river the streets are of gold. There are enjoyments and pleasures untold; Over the river time never grows old, Bearing the burden of years.

2 Over the river the streets are of gold,
There are enjoyments and pleasures untold;
Over the river time never grows old,
  Bearing the burden of years.
There all our sighing and sorrows shall cease,
Hush'd by the chorus of heavenly peace;
Over the river, thrice happy release,
  We shall be free from our fears.

3 There every tear shall be wiped from our eyes;
There, where the sunlight of glory ne'er dies,
Lighting forever those fair upper skies,
  Eden's glad plains to adorn.
Over the river, fair kingdom of light,
There heaven's mansions forever are bright;
Over the river there cometh no night,
  Long is eternity's morn.

4 Over the river, we've crossed it at last;
Over the river, our danger is passed;
Safe in the harbor our barks are moored fast,
  Ne'er from their haven to roam.
Then will we sing with the glorified throng,
Loud hallelujahs in one happy song;
Praising the power that has brought us along,
  Over the river at—home.

242. Beautiful Home.

FRANK FOREST. "Beautiful for situation is Zion." H. R. PALMER, by per.

1. There is a home e-ter-nal, Beau-ti-ful and bright, Where sweet joys su-per-nal Never are dimm'd by night; White-robed angels are singing, Ever around the bright throne, When, O when shall I see thee, Beau-ti-ful, beau-ti-ful home.

CHORUS.
Home, beauti-ful home, Bright, beauti-ful home, Home, home of our Sav-iour, Bright, beau-ti-ful home.
Beau-ti-ful home, Beau-ti-ful home, Beau-ti-ful, beauti-ful home.

2 Flowers forever are springing
In that home so fair,
Thousands of children are singing
Praises to Jesus there;
How they swell the glad anthems
Ever around the bright throne,
When, O when shall I see thee,
Beautiful, beautiful home?

3 Soon shall I join that anthem,
Far beyond the sky,
Jesus became my ransom;
Why should I fear to die?
Soon my eyes will behold him,
Seated upon the bright throne,
Then, O then shall I see thee,
Beautiful, beautiful home.

243. Fading Flower.

ANNE STEELE. "So death passed upon all."

1. When blooming youth is snatched a-way By death's re-sist-less hand, Our hearts the mournful tribute pay, Which pit-y must demand, Which pit-y must de-mand.

2 While pity prompts the rising sigh,
O, may this truth, impressed
With awful power, "I, too, must die,"
Sink deep in every breast.

3 Let this vain world engage no more;
Behold the opening tomb;

It bids us seize the present hour;
To-morrow death may come.

4 O, let us fly—to Jesus fly,
Whose powerful arm can save;
Then shall our hopes ascend on high,
And triumph o'er the grave.

244. Beyond the Sunset.

JOSEPHINE POLLARD. W. O. PERKINS, by per.

2 Beyond the sunset's purple rim,
Beyond the twilight deep and dim,
Where clouds and darkness never come,
My soul shall find its heavenly home.

3 Beyond this desert dark and drear,
The golden city will appear,
And morning's lovely beams arise
Upon my mansion in the skies.

4 Those golden portals ever shine
Beyond the reach of day's decline,
And Jesus bids my soul prepare
To gain a happy entrance there.

245. 'Neath Elim's Cooling Palms.

"And they came to Elim, where were twelve wells of water, and threescore and ten palm-trees."—Ex. 15:27.

B. F. BRISTOW. F. L. BRISTOW.

1. We are toiling onward hand in hand, (hand in hand,) We are toiling for the promised land; Come and join our weary pilgrim band, (pilgrim band,) We shall rest 'neath E-lim's cool-ing palms. Tho' the waves loudly roar, We shall pass safely o'er To the

'Neath Elim's Cooling Palms. Concluded.

2 By the swelling waters, clear and sweet,
After toiling through the desert's heat,
We shall rest our worn and weary feet,
   We shall rest 'neath Elim's cooling palms.

3 There will be no dark and dreary night,
We shall rest forever from the fight;
We shall dwell forever in the light,
   We shall rest 'neath Elim's cooling palms.

---

246   Beautiful Realm of Delight.

R. G. Staples.   M. J. Munger.

2 Have you heard of its streets that are paved with gold?
Beautiful realm of delight;
There the saints of all ages the face behold
Of their Saviour, who giveth it light.

3 Have you heard of its rivers—its crystal streams?
Beautiful realm of delight;
Of the sun that shines brightly, with healing beams,
Never setting in darkness of night.

4 All its walls are of jasper—of pearl its gates,
Beautiful realm of delight;
There a crown of rejoicing the saint awaits,
When he enters its "portals of light."

247. What a Gath'ring that will be.

J. H. K.   J. H. KURZENKNABE.

By permission of J. H. Kurzenknabe & Sons, Harrisburg, Pa.

1 At the sounding of the trumpet, when the saints are gather'd home,
   We will greet each other by the crystal sea;
  With the friends and all the lov'd ones there awaiting us to come,
   What a gath'ring of the faithful that will be!

2 When the angel of the Lord proclaims that time shall be no more,
   We shall gather, and the sav'd and ransom'd see;
  Then to meet again together, on the bright celestial shore,
   What a gath'ring of the faithful that will be!

3 At the great and final judgment, when the hidden comes to light,
   When the Lord in all his glory we shall see;
  At the bidding of our Saviour, "Come, ye blessed, to my right,"
   What a gath'ring of the faithful that will be!

4 When the golden harps are sounding, and the angel bands proclaim
   In triumphant strains the glorious jubilee;
  Then to meet and join to sing the song of Moses and the Lamb,
   What a gath'ring of the faithful that will be!

Land of the Blessed.

Mrs. Emily Huntington Miller. T. C. O'Kane, by per.

2 Oh! Land of the blessed, thy hills of delight
  Sometimes on my vision unfold;
Thy mansions celestial, thy palaces bright,
  Thy bulwarks of jasper and gold.
Dear voices are chanting thy chorus of praise,
  Dear eyes in thy sunlight are fair;
I look from my valley of shadow, below,
  And whisper: would God I were there!

3 Dear home of my Father, fair city, whose peace
  No shadow of changing can mar!
How glad are the souls that have tasted thy joy,
  How blest thine inhabitants are!
When weary with toiling, I think of the day—
  Who knows if its dawning be near?
When he who hath loved me shall call me away
  From all that hath burdened me here.

249. The Beautiful Shore.

"And there shall be no more death, neither sorrow, nor crying."—Rev. 21: 4.

MISS HATTIE BRONSON.　　　　　　　　　　　　WM. W. BENTLEY.

1. There's a home for the blest on the beau-ti-ful shore, Where our trials and cares all shall cease; Sorrow never shall en-ter that bliss-ful a-bode, Ev-er there shall a-bide per-fect peace.

CHORUS.

On that beautiful shore, Where the bright an-gels stay, All our sor-row and pain will be o'er; O, we long to go home to that beau-ti-ful land, There to rest, sweetly rest ev-er-more!

2 The bright streets of the city are paved with pure gold,
　And its flowers are fragrant and fair;
　Its inhabitants never grow weary nor old,
　For the Lord reigns eternally there.

3 There will be no more parting from those that we love,
　No more sighing or shedding of tears,
　For no discords shall ruffle that peaceful repose,
　Which flows through eternity's years.

4 O! we soon shall be called to that beautiful land,
　There to dwell with the just evermore;
　There to join in sweet songs with the friends that we love,
　Safe at home on the beautiful shore.

250. Home.

CHAS. H. GABRIEL.

Be-yond the smiling and the weep-ing, I shall be soon, Be-yond the wak-ing and the sleep-ing, Beyond the sow-ing and the reap-ing, I shall be soon.

Copyright, 1892, by Guide Printing & Publishing Co.

2 Beyond the blooming and the fading,
　I shall be soon,
Beyond the shining and the shading,
Beyond the hoping and the dreading,
　I shall be soon.

3 Beyond the parting and the meeting,
　I shall be soon,
Beyond the farewell and the greeting,
Beyond the pulse's fevered beating,
　I shall be soon.

251. The Great By-and-by.

REV. W. G. HASKELL. J. P. WEBSTER.

1. O, the years they are gliding away, And they bear all the children along! Let us never entreat them to stay, But speed them with smile and with song.

CHORUS.
In the great by-and-by, There'll be service we're willing to do; O, the great by-and-by Brings reward to the faithful and true.
by-and-by, by-and-by, In the great by-and-by.

2 We'll be women and men by-and-by,
Taking up all the burdens of life;
But with hearts beating hopefully high,
We'll go forth to the toil and the strife.
CHO. For the great by-and-by
Brings the harvest of joy to the soul;
O, the great by-and-by!
It will last while eternities roll.

3 O, the years they go fleeting away
T'ward the sun that shall never go down!
And the souls who are faithful to-day
Shall receive from the Father a crown.
CHO. In the great by-and-by,
When we meet all the loved gone before;
In the great by-and-by,
When we stand on eternity's shore.

Home. Concluded.

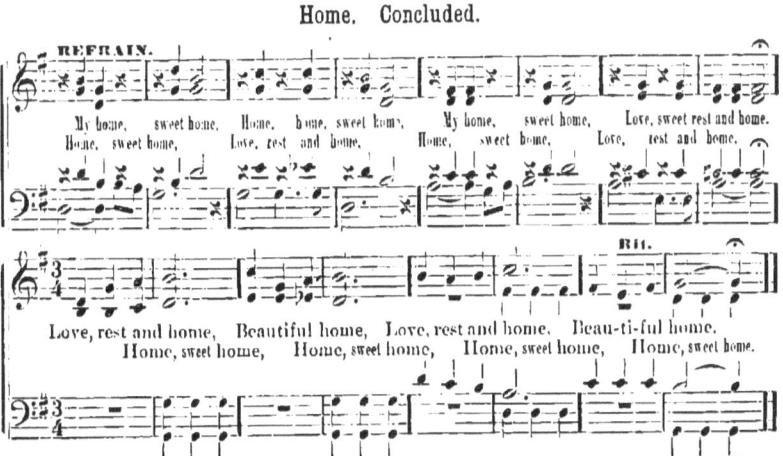

REFRAIN.
My home, sweet home, Home, home, sweet home, My home, sweet home, Love, sweet rest and home.
Home, sweet home, Love, rest and home, Home, sweet home, Love, rest and home.

Rit.
Love, rest and home, Beautiful home, Love, rest and home, Beautiful home.
Home, sweet home, Home, sweet home, Home, sweet home, Home, sweet home.

252. The Hope of the Soul.

W. P. Rivers.   R. M. McIntosh.

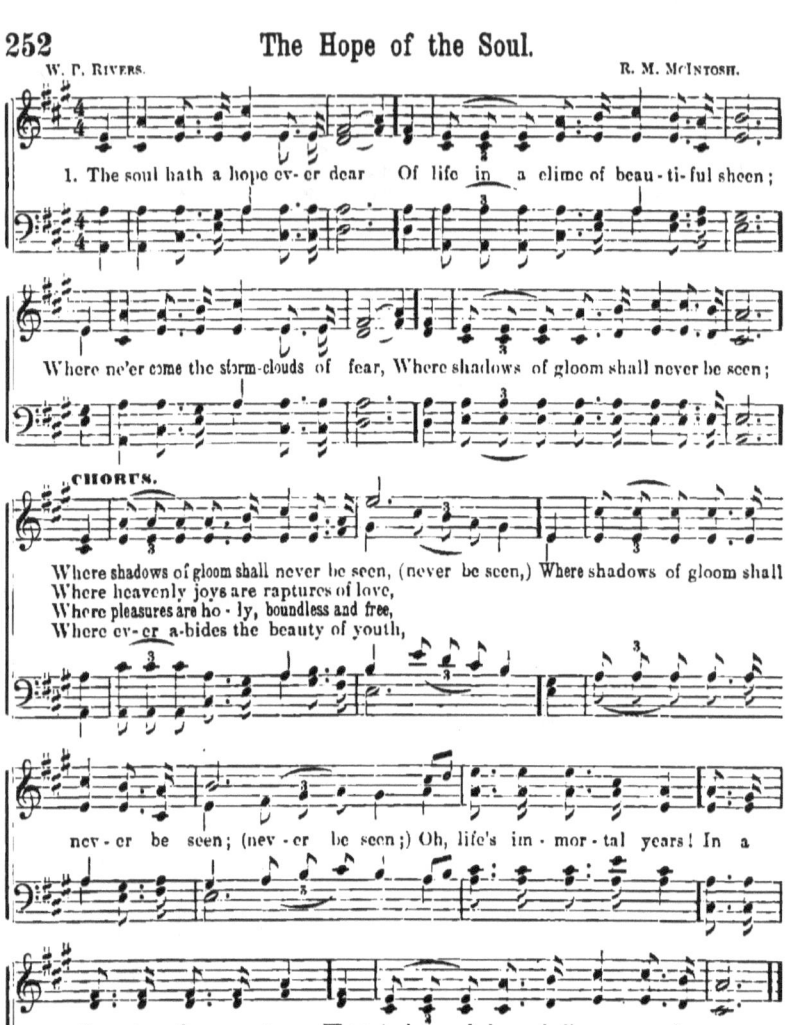

1. The soul hath a hope ev-er dear / Of life in a clime of beau-ti-ful sheen; / Where ne'er come the storm-clouds of fear, Where shadows of gloom shall never be seen;

CHORUS.
Where shadows of gloom shall never be seen, (never be seen,) Where shadows of gloom shall never be seen; (nev-er be seen;) Oh, life's im-mor-tal years! In a clime where flow no tears—Where shadows of gloom shall nev-er be seen.

Copyright, 1886, by R. M. McIntosh.

1 The soul hath a hope ever dear
  Of life in a clime of beautiful sheen;
Where ne'er come the storm-clouds of fear,
  Where shadows of gloom shall never be seen.

2 Sweet hope of the life ever blest
  With God in his home, with Jesus above;
Where angels and saints are at rest,
  Where heavenly joys are raptures of love.

3 Dear hope of the soul's better life—
  An ocean of Peace—sweet Purity's sea!
Where never is tempest or strife,
  Where pleasures are holy, boundless, and free.

4 O soul, keep thy hope ever pure,
  Of life in the clime of virtue and truth;
Where visions of glory endure,
  Where ever abides the beauty of youth.

253. By and By.

"And every eye shall see him."—Rev. 1:7 R. M. McIntosh, by per.

1 It may be far, it may be near,
There is a hope, there is a fear,
But in the future waiting, I
Shall Jesus see, yes, "by and by."

2 Impatient soul, and murm'ring heart,
Your murm'ring cease and bear your part
Of pain and labor on life's road,
For soon 'twill lead thee to thy God.

3 Yes, "by and by" will soon be now,"
And God shall wipe each tear-stain'd brow;
The Lamb shall feed them from the throne,
To living fountains lead his own.

4 Oh, verdant fields! oh, shining shore!
The Lamb of God spreads wide the door,
Ah! golden city, surely I
Shall see thy glories "by and by."

254. Patmos.

ANNE SHEPHERD.   W. E. MATHEWS.

2 What brought them to that world above,
That heaven so bright and fair,—
Where all is peace, and joy, and love?
How came those children there?

3 Because the Saviour shed his blood
To wash away their sins;
Bathed in that pure and precious flood,
Behold them white and clean!

255. Meet me There.

H. E. BLAIR. WM. J. KIRKPATRICK.

1. On the happy golden shore, Where the faithful part no more, When the storms of life are o'er, Meet me there. Where the night dissolves a-way, Into pure and perfect day, I am going home to stay, Meet me there.

CHORUS.
Meet me there, Meet me there, Where the tree of life is blooming, Meet me there, When the
Meet me there, Meet me there, Meet me there, Meet me there,

D. S.—*storms of life are o'er, On the happy golden shore, Where the faithful part no more, Meet me there.*

Copyright, 1885, by W. J. Kirkpatrick.

2 Here our fondest hopes are vain,
Dearest links are rent in twain:
But in heaven no throb of pain,
   Meet me there.
By the river sparkling bright,
In the city of delight,
Where our faith is lost in sight,
   Meet me there.

3 Where the harps of angels ring,
And the blest forever sing,
In the palace of the King,
   Meet me there.
Where in sweet communion blend
Heart with heart, and friend with friend,
In a world that ne'er shall end,
   Meet me there.

256. Round the Throne.

W. A. O. W. A. OGDEN.

1. There are little children singing round the throne, In that heav'nly land, In that heav'nly land; They are

CHORUS.
singing round the bright eternal throne, The great white throne of God. We shall meet them in their bright eternal home, We will

257. They Are Going Down the Valley.

MRS. C. L. SHACKLOCK.   FRANK M. DAVIS, by per.

1. They are going down the valley, the dim dark valley, We shall see their faces nevermore;
2. When the glory of the morning, the sky adorning, Floods the earth with sunshine, we shall mourn.

They are passing thro' the portal, the shad'wy portal, That leads to the Saviour we adore.
For the blossoms we have cherished, so fondly cherished, The blast from our loving clasp has torn.

REFRAIN.
They are going down the valley, the dim dark valley, For ev-er-more, for ev-er-more.

3 Upon us the shadow falleth, its gloom appalleth,
   For the light departed we shall weep,
But from the heights of love above us they still will love us,
   And o'er us a tender vigil keep.

4 And when we too pass the portal of life immortal,
   When our bark shall anchor on the shore,
Oh, how sweet will be the greeting, the joyous greeting,
   When we meet our beloved once more!

Round the Throne.—Concluded.

sing with them round the great white throne; We will sing of him who died, Of our Saviour crucified, Round the great white throne of God.

2 There are angels, happy angels round the throne,
   In that heavenly land, in that heavenly land;
They are happy round the bright, eternal throne,
   The great white throne of God.

3 We are little children, striving for the throne,
   In that heavenly land, in that heavenly land;
We are striving for that bright, eternal throne,
   The great white throne of God.

4 We are marching onward, marching to the throne,
   In that heavenly land, in that heavenly land;
Come and join us in our journey to the throne,
   The great white throne of God.

CHORUS FOR LAST VERSE ONLY.
We will gather in our bright eternal home;
We will shout his praises round the "great white throne!"
We will sing of him who died, etc.

258. He's Watching O'er Me.

J. C. B.   J. CALVIN BUSHEY.

The Saviour is watching by night and by day, Where'er we roam, And tenderly follows wherever we stray,

CHORUS.

And brings us home. Yes, Jesus my Saviour, is watching o'er me, Is watching o'er me wherever I roam; Yes, Jesus my Saviour, is watching o'er me, And calling me, calling me home.
Yes, Je - sus is

Copyright, 1866, by R. M. McIntosh.

2 While here upon earth little children could come
   And share his love;
And now he has gone to prepare them a home
   In heav'n above.

3 My song shall forever and evermore be
   To him above,
Who came down to save a poor sinner like me,
   Oh! wondrous love!

259. I Have a Sweet Hope.

J. H. MARTIN.   Dr. A. B. EVERETT, by per.

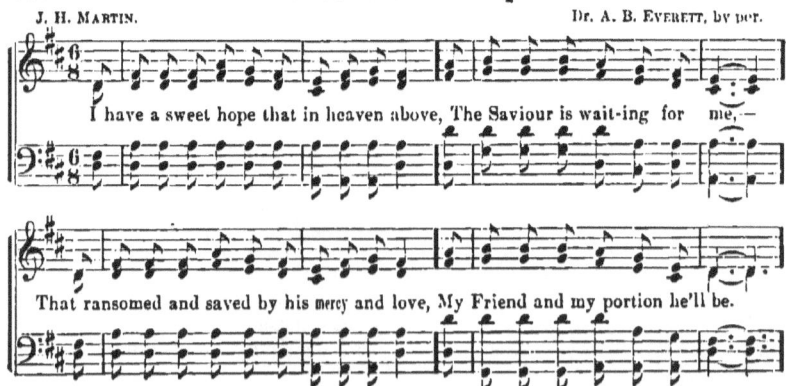

I have a sweet hope that in heaven above, The Saviour is wait-ing for me,—
That ransomed and saved by his mercy and love, My Friend and my portion he'll be.

260   I am Waiting.

J. G.   JOSEPH GARRISON.

1. I am waiting for Jesus to welcome me home, To the place he has gone to prepare, To the mansion of light and the

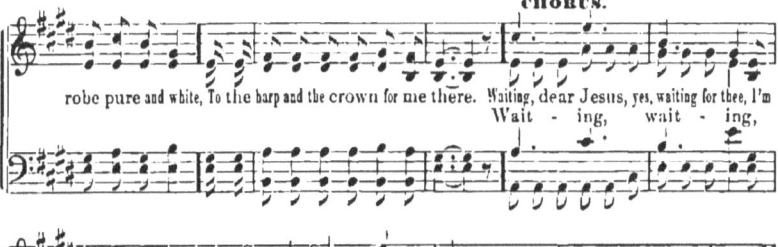

robe pure and white, To the harp and the crown for me there. Waiting, dear Jesus, yes, waiting for thee, I'm
                                          Wait - ing,   wait - ing,

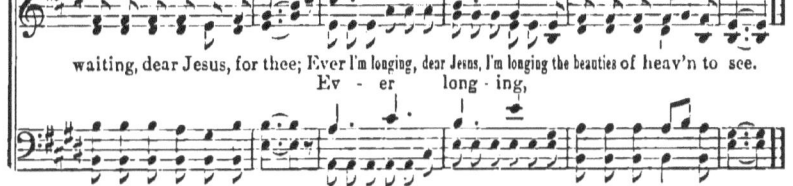

waiting, dear Jesus, for thee; Ever I'm longing, dear Jesus, I'm longing the beauties of heav'n to see.
                  Ev - er   long - ing,

2 Many loved ones have I in that beautiful land,
    They are watching and waiting for me,
    And they beckon me o'er to that bright happy shore,
    There the beauties of glory to see.

3 Roll along, then, sweet moments, and bear me away
    To my beautiful home in the sky,
    To the land of the blest, where I sweetly shall rest,
    In the palace of Jesus on high.

I Have a Sweet Hope.   Concluded.

Jesus, dear Jesus will welcome me, Welcome me, welcome me; Jesus, dear Jesus will welcome me Home to the beautiful land.

2 In midst of the troubles and sorrows I bear,
    By faith I repose on his breast:
   I know he will make my afflictions his care,
    And bring me at last to his rest.
3 He's going to prepare for his people a place,—
    A mansion of glory on high;

   And when I shall finish my journey and race,
    He'll give me a home in the sky.
4 I know when this body of flesh shall decay,
    My Strength and my Portion he'll be:
   In death he will be my sweet Comfort and Stay,
    The Saviour is waiting for me.

261. In the Harbor.

JESSIE H. BROWN. ALEX. C. HOPKINS.

1. After the voyage and the water's mad riot, After the tempests that break on the sea,
Blessed the port where we anchor in qui-et, Blessed the rest in the harbor for me.

CHORUS.

Blessed the rest in the har-bor for me, Blessed the rest in the har-bor for me,
Blessed the port where we enter in qui-et, Bless-ed the rest in the har-bor for me.

Copyright, 1887, by Fillmore Bros.

2 Blessed the thought that the voyaging is over,
Blessed the thought that the voyager is free;
Home is awaiting the travel-worn rover,
Lights in that harbor are shining for me.

3 When the long voyage of this life shall be ended,
Thus we shall anchor beyond the rough sea,
Lights which the angels of heaven have tended
Shine from the harbor for you and for me.

262. Watching for Me.

HENRIETTA E. BLAIR. WM. J. KIRKPATRICK.

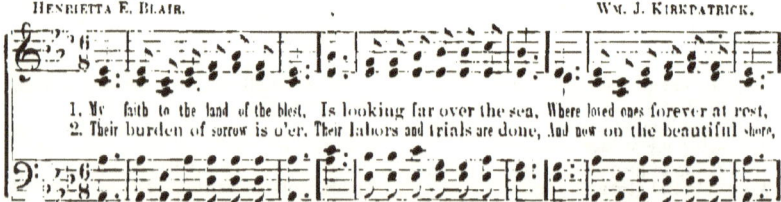

1. My faith to the land of the blest, Is looking far over the sea, Where loved ones forever at rest,
2. Their burden of sorrow is o'er, Their labors and trials are done, And now on the beautiful shore,

Watching for Me.—Concluded.

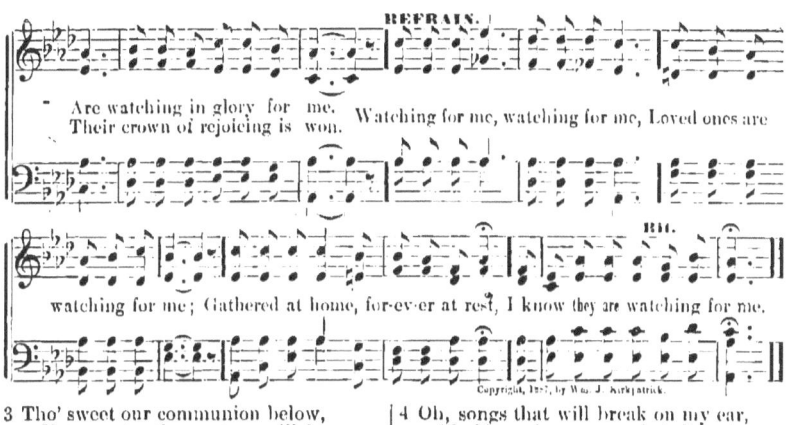

3 Tho' sweet our communion below,
Yet sweeter the rapture will be
When called by the Saviour to go
Where loved ones are watching for me.

4 Oh, songs that will break on my ear,
Oh, bliss when my soul shall be free,
And meet by the river so clear,
The friends that are watching for me.

263 Is it Written There?

J. E. RANKIN. E. S. LORENZ.

3 I do not ask that my earthly life
Should be free from burdens, and cares and strife;
Nor that its current have tranquil flow,
If but this one thing I may surely know:

4 I'd give up all that I hope below,
All that time can give or the world bestow,
If when the Lord in his kingdom come,
He will know me then, and will take me home.

264. The Land of Beulah.

Rev. SIDNEY S. BREWSTER. Arranged.

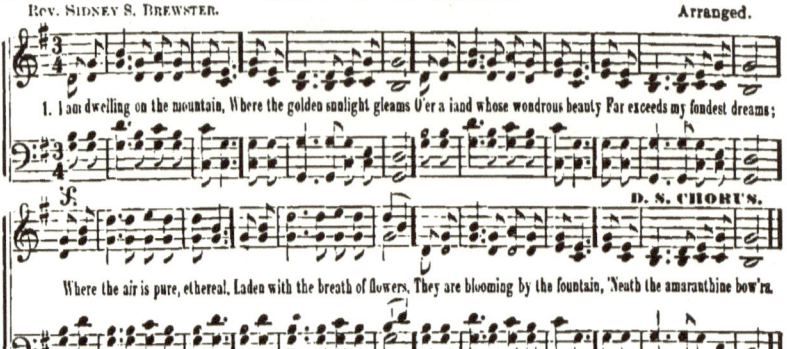

1. I am dwelling on the mountain, Where the golden sunlight gleams O'er a land whose wondrous beauty Far exceeds my fondest dreams;

Where the air is pure, ethereal, Laden with the breath of flowers, They are blooming by the fountain, 'Neath the amaranthine bow'rs.

Cho.—Is not this the land of Beulah, Blessed, blessed land of light, Where the flowers bloom forever, And the sun is always bright.

2 I can see far down the mountain,
Where I wandered weary years,
Often hindered in my journey
By the ghosts of doubts and fears,
Broken vows and disappointments
Thickly sprinkled all the way,
But the Spirit led, unerring,
To the land I hold to-day.

3 I am drinking at the fountain,
Where I ever would abide;
For I've tasted life's pure river,
And my soul is satisfied;
There's no thirsting for life's pleasures,
Nor adorning, rich and gay,
For I've found a richer treasure,
One that fadeth not away.

4 Tell me not of heavy crosses,
Nor the burdens hard to bear,
For I've found this great salvation
Makes each burden light appear;
And I love to follow Jesus,
Gladly counting all but dross,
Worldly honors all forsaking
For the glory of the Cross.

5 Oh, the Cross has wondrous glory!
Oft I've proved this to be true;
When I'm in the way so narrow,
I can see a pathway through;
And how sweetly Jesus whispers:
Take the Cross, thou need'st not fear,
For I've tried the way before thee,
And the glory lingers near.

265. There is a Happy Land.

1. There is a hap-py land, Far, far a-way, Where saints in glo-ry stand, Bright, bright as day;

O, how they sweet-ly sing, Worth-y is our Sav-iour-King, Loud let his prais-es ring, Praise, praise for aye.

2 Come to that happy land,
Come, come away;
Why will ye doubting stand,
Why still delay?
O, we shall happy be,
When, from sin and sorrow free,
Lord, we shall live with thee,
Blest, blest for aye.

3 Bright, in that happy land,
Beams ev'ry eye;
Kept by a Father's hand,
Love can not die.
O, then to glory run,
Be a crown and kingdom won;
And bright above the sun,
We reign for aye.

"Out of the mouths of babes and sucklings hast thou perfected praise."— Matt. 21: 16.

270   Come Away to the Sunday-School.

FRANK M. DAVIS, by per.

2 How we love the meetings there, in our blessed Sunday-School,
   Come away, come away, come away;
 There unite in praise and prayer, at our Father's gracious call,
   Come away, come away, come away;
 There we've teachers, kind and true, come away,
 There we've books, both old and new, come away,
 There we love to heed each rule, in our pleasant Sunday-School,
   Come away, come away, come away.

3 There we learn of Jesus' love, in our blessed Sunday-School,
   Come away, come away, come away,
 And the road that leads above, where there's happiness for all,
   Come away, come away, come away;
 There we sing our songs of love, come away,
 And are taught of things above, come away,
 Then let 's heed the cheerful call, for the blessed Sunday-School,
   Come away, come away, come away.

271. The Sunday-School Army.

2 Fight on, ye little soldiers,
  The battle you shall win,
  Fight on, ye little soldiers,
  The battle you shall win;
  For the Saviour is your Captain,
  For the Saviour is your Captain,
  And he hath vanquished sin.

3 And when the conflict's over,
  Before him you shall stand;
  And when the conflict's over,
  Before him you shall stand;
  You shall sing his praise forever,
  You shall sing his praise forever,
  In Canaan's happy land.

272. Gather Them In.

273 When the Morning Light.

2 On the frosty dawn of a winter's morn,
  When the earth is wrapped in snow,
Or the summer's breeze plays around the trees,
  To the Sunday-School I go;
When the holy day has come,
And the Sabbath-breakers roam,
I delight to leave my home,
  For the Sunday-School.

3 In the class I meet with the friends I greet,
  At the time of morning prayer,
And our hearts we raise in a hymn of praise,
  For 't is always pleasant there.
In the Book of holy truth,
Full of counsel and reproof,
We behold the guide of youth,
  At the Sunday-School.

4 May the dews of grace fill the hallowed place,
  And the sunshine never fail,
While each blooming rose which in memory grows,
  Shall a sweet perfume exhale.
When we mingle here no more,
But have met on Jordan's shore,
We will talk of moments o'er,
  At the Sunday-School.

Gather Them In. Concluded.

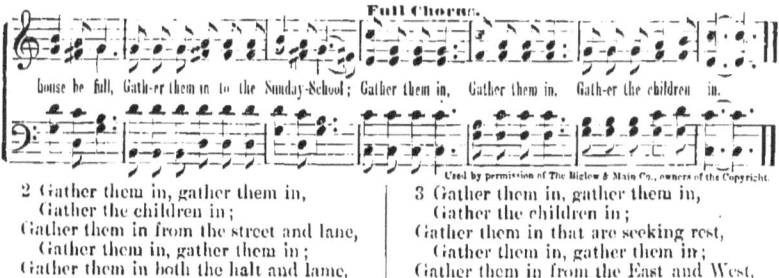

Used by permission of The Bigelow & Main Co., owners of the Copyright.

2 Gather them in, gather them in,
  Gather the children in;
Gather them in from the street and lane,
  Gather them in, gather them in;
Gather them in both the halt and lame,
  Gather, gather them in;
Gather the deaf, and the poor, and blind,
  Gather them in, gather them in;
Gather them in with a willing mind,
  Gather, gather them in.

3 Gather them in, gather them in,
  Gather the children in;
Gather them in that are seeking rest,
  Gather them in, gather them in;
Gather them in from the East and West,
  Gather, gather them in;
Gather them in that are roaming about,
  Gather them in, gather them in;
Gather them in from the North and South,
  Gather, gather them in.

274. "This Grand Little Army."

"Feed the flock of God, which is among you."—1 Peter 5: 2.

Mrs. Harriet Jones.   M. J. Munger.

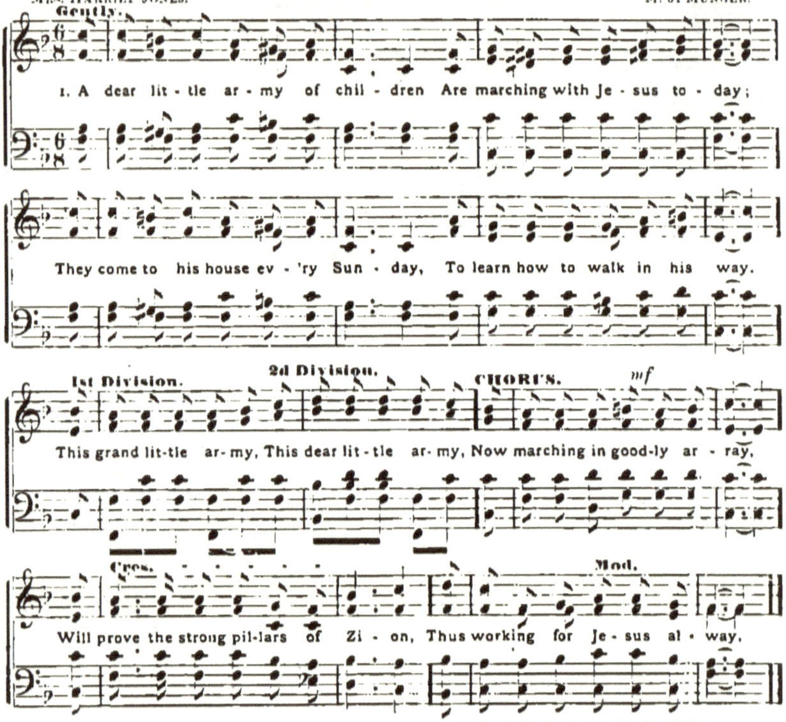

1. A dear lit-tle ar-my of chil-dren Are marching with Je-sus to-day;
They come to his house ev-'ry Sun-day, To learn how to walk in his way.

Chorus.
This grand lit-tle ar-my, This dear lit-tle ar-my, Now marching in good-ly ar-ray,
Will prove the strong pil-lars of Zi-on, Thus working for Je-sus al-way.

2 O, sweet is the task of the teacher
While leading the dear little band,
O, sweet is the smile of the Saviour
While viewing the work of your hand.

3 He surely will smile on the teacher,
Who keepeth from going astray
The feet of the dear little children,
Who march in his army to-day.

4 And O, how he loves little children,
While sweetly they learn how to do
The things that are taught in the Bible,
The Bible so precious and true.

5 March on, little army of Jesus!
Sometime in the "Sweet By-and-by,"
Your work shall be felt by the nation,
Your names shall be written on high.

275. Loving Each Other.

E. S. Lorenz.   *"Let us love one another."*—1 John 4:1.   E. S. Lorenz.

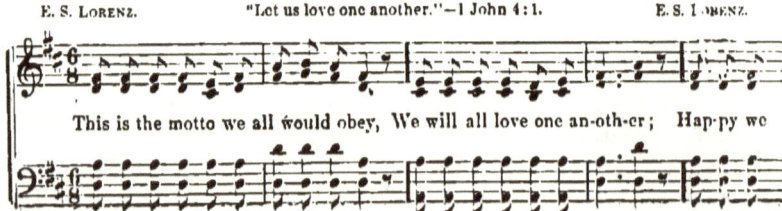

This is the motto we all would obey, We will all love one an-oth-er; Hap-py we

Loving Each Other.—Concluded.

2 Thus will we labor and thus will we play,
Trying to help one another;
Driving the sorrows of others away,
Bringing sweet peace to each other.

3 Let us, like Jesus, be thoughtful and kind,
Striving to please one another;
Here, as in heav'n, we will be of one mind,
Ev'ry one loving the other.

276 Little by Little.

MRS. CHAS. BARNARD.

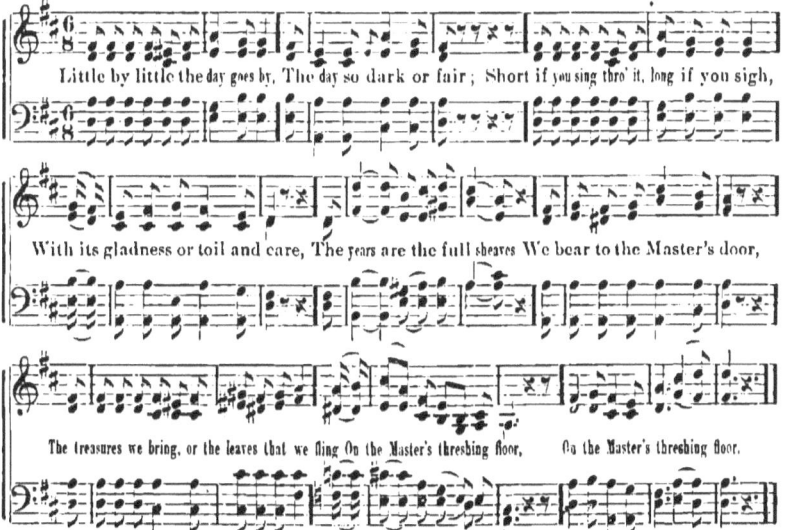

2 Little by little the skies grow clear, spring-buds come smiling out;
Little by little the sun shines near, the brighter for pain and doubt,—
A bloom of radiant beauty, that bridle or shrine might know,
Which, gone with the May that has vanished away, to fruitage most rare may grow.

3 Little by little the world grows strong, upborne by the good to men,
Fighting the battle of right against wrong, seen far beyond mortal ken ;
Brave souls ne'er are wanting, full arm'd for the deadly strife,
What tho' demons may rage, as the contest they wage, the crown is immortal life.

277. O Come, Come Away.

Allegro. — W. E. Hickson.

1. Oh, come, come away! the Lord's Day morn is passing, Let's hasten to the Sunday school; Oh, come, come away, 'The chiming bells are ringing clear, Their joyous peals salute my ear, I love their voice to hear, Oh, come, come away.

1 Oh, come, come away! the Lord's-Day morn is passing;
Let's hasten to the Sunday school; oh, come, &c.
The chiming bells are ringing clear,
Their joyous peals salute my ear,
I love their voice to hear; oh, come, &c.

2 Your comrads invite to join our happy number,
And gladly will I meet them there; oh, come, &c.
'Tis there we meet to sing and pray,
To read God's word on his glad day,
With joy let's haste away; oh, come, &c.

3 While others may seek for vain and foolish pleasures,
The Sunday school shall be my choice; oh, come, &c.
How dear to hear the plaintive strain,
From youthful voices rise amain,
With sweetest tones again! oh, come, &c.

4 'Tis there I may learn the ways of heavenly wisdom
To guide my feeble steps on high; oh, come, &c.
The flow'ry paths of peace to tread,
Where rays of heavenly bliss are shed,
My wand'ring steps to lead; oh, come, &c.

5 I there hear the voice in heavenly accents speaking,
"Let little children come to me; oh, come, &c.
Forbid them not their hearts to give,
Let them on me in youth believe,
And I will them receive;" oh, come, &c.

6 With joy I accept the gracious invitation,
My heart exults with rapturous hope; oh, come, &c.
My deathless spirit when I die,
Shall, on the wings of angels, fly
To mansions in the sky; oh, come, &c.

278. Come to Sunday-School.

Grace Glenn. — J. H. F.

1. Come while the grass in the path we tread Glistens with dew-drops so pearly; Hurry with me to the Sunday-school, So we may always be early.

2 Let us be quietly seated there
When the bell ceases its ringing,
Then we shall never disturb the pray'r,
But with the rest join in singing.

Every word of our lessons learned,
Careful shall be our behavior,
Listening well as our teacher dear
Tells us of Jesus, our Saviour.

279. Alleluia! Sweetly Sing.

J. M. NEALE.　　　　　　　　　　　　　　　　FREDERIC ALLDRED.

All is bright and cheerful round us, All above is soft and blue; Ev-'ry flow'r is full of gladness, Summer hath brought its pleasures too! Heavenly blessings! Showers of blessings! On our heads the dear Lord sends; Alle-luia, sweetly sing, Unto Christ, our heav'nly King!

Copyright, 1891, by Hunt & Eaton.

1 All is bright and cheerful round us,
 All above is soft and blue!
Every flower is full of gladness,
 Summer hath brought its pleasures too!

2 There are leaves that never wither,
 There are flowers that ne'er decay,
Nothing evil goeth thither,
 Nothing good is kept away.

280. See, Israel's Gentle Shepherd Stands.

PHILIP DODDRIDGE.　　　　　　　　　　　　WILLIAM V. WALLACE.

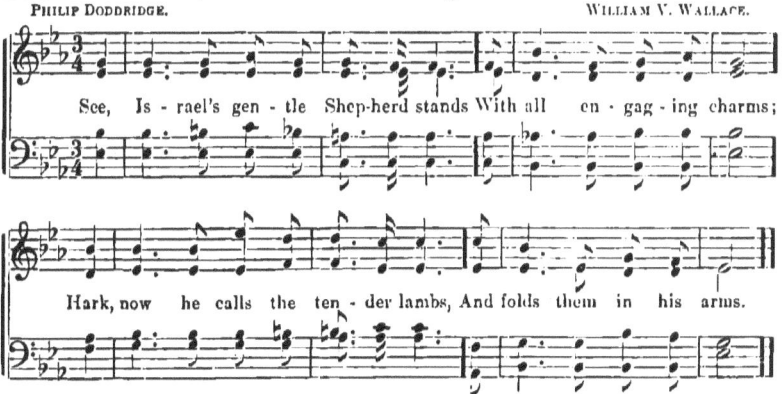

See, Is-rael's gen-tle Shep-herd stands With all en-gag-ing charms; Hark, now he calls the ten-der lambs, And folds them in his arms.

2 "Permit them to approach," he cries,
 "Nor scorn their humble name;
For 'twas to bless such souls as these
 The Lord of angels came."

3 We bring them, Lord, in thankful hands,
 And yield them up to thee;
Joyful that we ourselves are thine,
 Thine let our offspring be.

281. O Come, Little Children.

I. B.   "Suffer the little children to come unto me."—MARK 10: 14.   I. BALTZELL, by per.

1. O come, lit-tle chil-dren, your Sav-iour is call-ing, O come, in the morn-ing of vig-or and youth;
O come, while his blessings a-round you are fall-ing, O come, lit-tle ones, to the fount-ain of truth.

CHORUS.
O come to the Sav-iour, come, ask his kind fa-vor, And o-ver the riv-er you'll live ev-er-more.

2 O children, your Saviour is pleading in glory,
   O, hear him, obey him, your days may be few;
O, hear him repeating the ever-blest story,
   "O, come to me, children, I'm your Saviour too."

3 Then come to the Saviour, don't wait for the morrow,
   How many have waited, and saw not the day;
And now in the regions of darkness and sorrow
   They sadly remember, 'twas only delay.

282. I Will Follow Thee.

GRACE GLENN.   J. H. ROSECRANS.

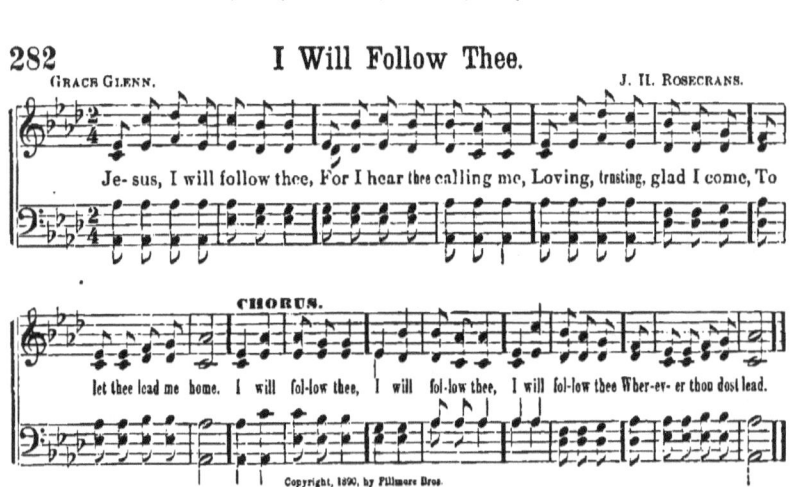

Je-sus, I will follow thee, For I hear thee calling me, Loving, trusting, glad I come, To let thee lead me home.

CHORUS.
I will fol-low thee, I will fol-low thee, I will fol-low thee Wher-ev-er thou dost lead.

Copyright, 1890, by Fillmore Bros.

1 Jesus, I will follow thee,
  For I hear thee calling me,
  Loving, trusting, glad I come,
  To let thee lead me home.

2 Little eyes might lose the way,
  Little feet might go astray,
  I might weak and weary be,
  But thou art strong for me.

3 Grief and want may be my foes,
  Foolish sins my way oppose,
  Full of courage I will be,
  Whene'er I follow thee.

283. All the Way.

FRANK M. DAVIS.   FRANK M. DAVIS.

1. All the way the Saviour leads me, All the way, all the way. All my needs he doth supply me, All the way, all the way; And his goodness faileth nev-er; He is mine, yes, mine forever; From his love I ne'er can sev-er, All the way, all the way.

By permission.

2 All the way the Saviour leads me,
All the way, all the way;
With the heavenly manna feeds me,
All the way, all the way.
Though the path be dark and dreary,
And my feet have grown so weary,
Yet he makes life seem so cheery,
All the way, all the way.

3 All the way the Saviour leads me,
All the way, all the way;
To the living waters guides me,
All the way, all the way.
What care I for earthly treasure,
What care I for worldly pleasure?
I have grace beyond the measure,
All the way, all the way.

284. Our Heavenly Guide.

C. H. PAYNE.   S. V. R. FORD.

1. O guide to rich-est treasures, In all the land and sea, Lead us to purest pleasures, We'll gladly follow thee. We come in youth's bright morning, And give to thee life's best; All e-vil ev-er scorn-ing, All good shall be our quest.

Copyright, 1891, by Hunt & Eaton.

2 Our being and our blessing
Are from thy bounteous hand;
Our sinfulness confessing,
We'll serve at thy command.
Accept the gifts we offer,
Defend us by thy might;
Use all the powers we proffer
In service of the right.

3 Our lives, enthroning Duty,
And radiant in its light,
Shall be "a thing of beauty,"
All jubilant and bright.
Our way shall ne'er be dreary
With thy dear presence blest;
Our hearts shall ne'er grow weary
Till toil shall end in rest.

285. Little Pilgrims.

"For here we have no continuing city, but we seek one to come."—HEB. 13:14.

ANNA SHAW.   J. H. ANDERSON.

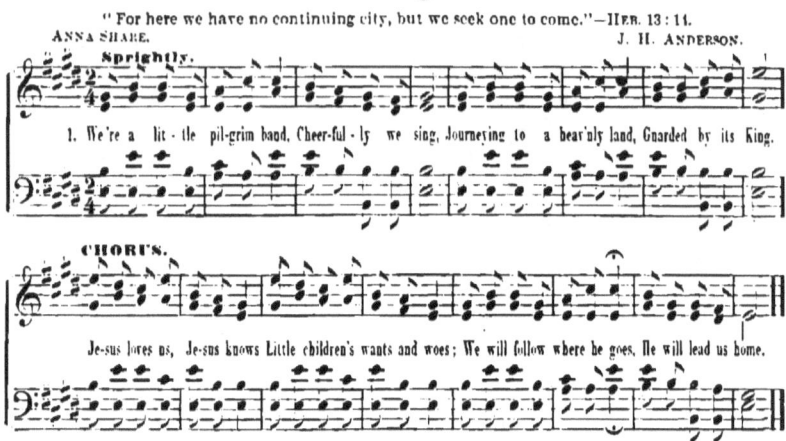

1. We're a lit-tle pil-grim band, Cheer-ful-ly we sing, Journeying to a heav'nly land, Guarded by its King.

CHORUS.

Je-sus loves us, Je-sus knows Little children's wants and woes; We will follow where he goes, He will lead us home.

Copyright, 1876, by REV. W. J. SHUEY.

2 Why should even children fear,
With a friend so true?
Pleasant is our pathway here,
Bright the end in view.

3 Ever onward, day by day,
Turning not aside,
Sure that in this narrow way,
Harm can ne'er betide.

4 We're a little pilgrim band,
Journeying with our King
To the shining better land—
This the song we sing.

286. Christmas Morning.

1. Lit-tle chil-dren, can you tell? Do you know the sto-ry well? Ev-ery girl and ev-ery boy, Why the an-gels sing for joy On the Christmas morn-ing?

2 Yes, we know the story well;
Listen now, and hear us tell,
Every girl and every boy,
Why the angels sing for joy
On the Christmas morning.

3 Shepherds sat upon the ground,
Fleecy flocks were scattered round,
When a brightness filled the sky,
And a song was heard on high
On the Christmas morning.

4 "Joy and peace," the angels sang,
Far the pleasant echoes rang;
"Peace on earth! to men good-will,"
Hark! the angels sing it still
On the Christmas morning.

5 For a little babe that day
Cradled in a manger lay;
Born on earth our Lord to be;
This the wondering angels see
On the Christmas morning.

6 Joy our little hearts shall fill,
Peace and love, and all good-will;
This fair babe of Bethlehem
Children loves, and blesses them
On the Christmas morning.

287. Beautiful the Little Hands.

T. CORBEN, D. D.   R. G. STAPLES.

1. Beau-ti-ful the lit-tle hands That fulfill the Lord's commands; Beau-ti-ful the lit-tle eyes, Kindled with light from the skies. Beau-ti-ful, beau-ti-ful lit-tle hands, That ful-fill the Lord's commands, (Omit. . . . .) Kin-dled with light from the skies.
2. All the lit-tle hands were made, Jesus' precious cause to aid; All the lit-tle hearts to beat Warm in his service so sweet. Beau-ti-ful, beau-ti-ful lit-tle eyes, (Omit. . . . .)

From Loving Voices.

3 All the little lips should pray
To the Saviour every day;
All the little feet should go,
Swift on his errands below.

4 What your little hands can do,
That the Lord intends for you;
Make that thing your first delight,
Do it to him with your might.

288. Bless Us and Keep us.

JULIA H. JOHNSTON.   FRANK M. DAVIS. By per.

1. Safely thro' another year, Thou hast brought each little one; Saviour, keep us in thy fear, Till our work shall all be done. Bless us and keep us, Bless us and keep us; Lord, bless and keep us, Till all our work is done.
2. For thy love and tender care, We would praise thy holy name; All thy goodness still we share, Jesus, ever-more the same.

Copyright, 1892, by R. M. McIntosh.

3 Thou hast watched and thou hast kept,
By thine own almighty arm;
In the dark while others slept,
Thou hast saved from fear and harm.

4 Lord, be with us through the year,
Let us hear thy tender voice;
May we feel thee ever near,
In thy love may we rejoice.

289. Now I Lay Me Down to Sleep.

"But thou, when thou prayest, enter into thy closet, * * *; and thy Father which seeth in secret shall reward thee openly."—MATT. 6: 6.

A. J. A.

1. Kneeling by her lit-tle bed-side, Dimpled feet so white and bare; Hands up-on her bo-som fold-ed, Hear her lisp her even-ing pray'r. Now I lay me down to sleep, I pray thee, Lord, my soul to keep.

2 In his arms he safely held me
Through the long and happy day;
And when night's uncertain shadows
Folded round her, she could say:
Ref.—If I should die before I wake,
I pray thee, Lord, my soul to take.

3 Like this little one, my Saviour,
Let me come to thee to-night;
Through the dark and silent watches,
Guide me to the morning light;
Ref.—Take me to thy loving breast,
And fold me in thine arms to rest.

4 On thy love alone depending,
Lead me to the life divine;
Let the prayer of trusting childhood
In the fullest sense be mine;
Ref.—If I wake or if I sleep,
'T is thou alone my soul must keep.

290. Little Soldiers.

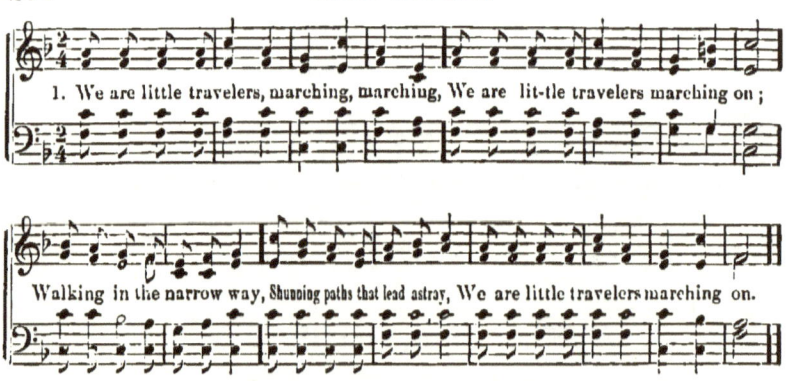

1. We are little travelers, marching, marching, We are lit-tle travelers marching on; Walking in the narrow way, Shunning paths that lead astray, We are little travelers marching on.

2 We are little laborers, working, working,
We are little laborers working on;
Never idling time away,
We are working all the day,
We are little laborers working on.

3 We are little soldiers, fighting, fighting,
We are little soldiers fighting on;
Warring 'gainst the pow'rs of sin,
Foes without and foes within,
We are little soldiers fighting on.

4 We are little pilgrims, hoping, hoping,
We are little pilgrims hoping on;
For a country better far,
Where our crown and kingdom are,
We are little pilgrims hoping on.

291   "Jesus Bids Us Shine."

MRS. EMILY HUNTINGTON MILLER.   WM. J. KIRKPATRICK.

Copyright, 1885, by W. J. KIRKPATRICK.

2 Jesus bids us shine, first of all for him,
Well he sees and knows it if our lights are dim
He looks down from heaven to see us shine,
You in your little corner, and I in mine.

3 Jesus bids us shine, then, for all around
Many kinds of darkness in this world are found;
Sin, and want, and sorrow; so we may shine,
You in your little corner, and I in mine.

292   Little Feet be Careful.

MRS. L. M. B. BATEMAN.   J. H. ROSECRANS.

Copyright, 1886, by Fillmore Bros.

2 I told my ears to listen
  Quite closely all day thro',
For any act of kindness,
  Such little hands can do.

3 My eyes are set to watch them
  About their work or play,
To keep them out of mischief,
  For Jesus' sake all day.

293. Friend of Children, Hear.

G. DEWSE.   GEORGE S. WEEKS.

1. Thou who once with man didst dwell, Thou whose tendr'st accents fell, When the little ones drew near, Jesus, friend of children, hear.

Now in youth's fair morning hour, Whilst the dew is on the flow'r, Er - er, Sav-iour, be thou near, Je-sus, friend of children, hear.

Copyright, 1875, by George S. Weeks.

2 When by parents, pastors taught,
Check, O Lord, each wand'ring tho't ;
Teach us reverence and fear,
Jesus, our petitions hear.
When in after years we roam
Far from teachers, far from home,
Guide us, guard us, Saviour dear,
Jesus, friend of children, hear.

3 If success in life be ours,
All our path be strewn with flowers,
In our happiness be near,
"Light of Light," in mercy hear.

Or if poverty's low cot,
Pain or suffering be our lot,
Thou the drooping heart canst cheer,
Friend of mourners, then be near.

4 If preserved to hoary age,
Keep us in life's latest stage ;
When the gate of death is near,
Lighten thou the passage drear.
Then when life's brief course is run,
Thou our hope, our shield, our sun,
Like to thee may we appear,
Jesus, Saviour, hear, oh, hear.

294. Looking Unto Jesus.

A. P. COBB.   A. C. HOPKINS.

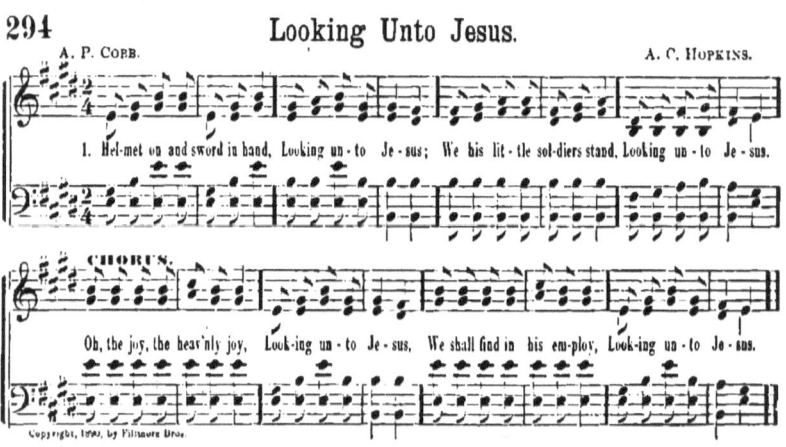

1. Hel-met on and sword in hand, Looking un-to Je-sus; We his lit-tle sol-diers stand, Looking un-to Je-sus.

CHORUS.

Oh, the joy, the heav'nly joy, Look-ing un-to Je-sus, We shall find in his em-ploy, Look-ing un-to Je-sus.

Copyright, 1880, by Fillmore Bros.

2 Faith our shield, and girt with truth,
Looking unto Jesus;
Serving him in joyous youth,
Looking unto Jesus.

3 Fiery darts on ev'ry hand,
Looking unto Jesus;

Daring all, we still shall stand,
Looking unto Jesus.

4 Praying always, with all pray'r,
Looking unto Jesus;
Watching thereunto with care,
Looking unto Jesus.

295. Sailing O'er the Sea.

I. B. — I. BALTZELL, by per.

1 We're a happy pilgrim band,
Sailing to the goodly land,
With a swelling sail we onward sweep;
Tho' the tempest rages long,
There is One among the throng,
Who will guide us safely o'er the deep.

2 When the mighty billows swell,
With the saved it shall be well,
Tho' the breakers roar upon the lea;
Rolling waves shall not o'erwhelm,
For we've Jesus at the helm,
And he'll guide us safely o'er the sea.

296. Thou Art My Shepherd.

Miss ELSIE THALHEIMER. — German.

297. The Bible Says I May.

"Fight the good fight of faith; lay hold on eternal life."—1 TIM. 6:12.   JUDSON.

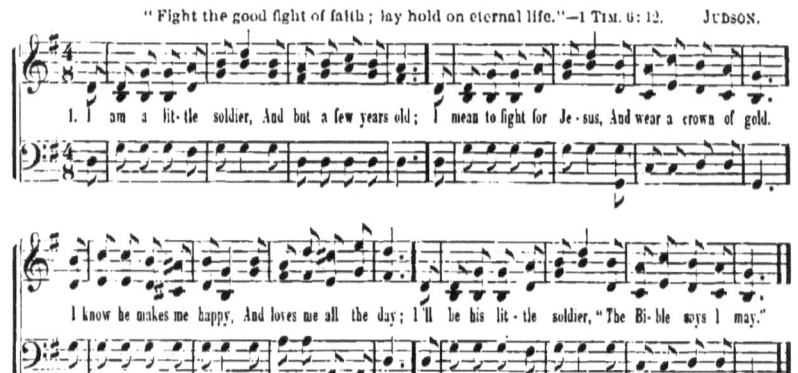

1. I am a lit-tle soldier, And but a few years old; I mean to fight for Je-sus, And wear a crown of gold. I know he makes me happy, And loves me all the day; I'll be his lit-tle soldier, "The Bi-ble says I may."

2 I love my precious Saviour,
  Because he died for me;
  And if I did not serve him,
  How sinful I should be!
  He gives me every comfort,
  And hears me when I pray;
  I want to live for Jesus,
  "The Bible says I may."

3 I now can do but little,
  Yet when I grow a man,
  I'll try and do for Jesus
  The greatest good I can.
  God help and keep me faithful
  In all I do or say;
  I want to live a Christian,
  "The Bible says I may."

298. We are Marching.

MRS. MATILDA C. EDWARDS.   R. M. McINTOSH.

1. We are marching to the kingdom, A little pilgrim band, And our Captain walks before us, To guide us thro' the land.

CHORUS.
We are marching, we are marching, We are marching to the kingdom, We are marching to the kingdom, A little pilgrim band.

2 We have just begun the battle,
  We are fighting for the crown;
  And we mean to gain the victory
  Ere we lay our armor down.

3 We have brothers gone before us,
  To join the white-robed band;
  O, how glad they'll be to see us
  Safe in that happy land!

4 They are waiting for our coming
  On that bright blessed shore;
  And how sweet 't will be to meet them
  Where parting is no more.

5 March on, dear little pilgrims,
  March on and take your crown;
  And bear your cross with patience,
  Till called to lay it down.

299. Happy Beulah Land.

"Here we have no continuing city, but we seek one to come."—HEB. 13:14.

D. B. P.   D. B. PURINTON.

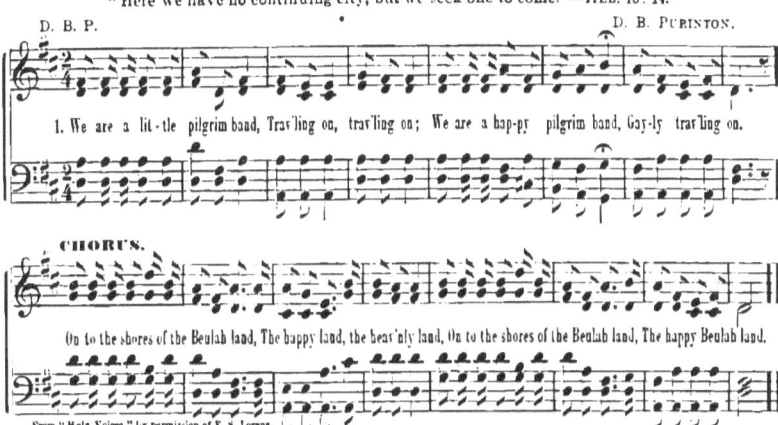

1. We are a lit-tle pilgrim band, Trav'ling on, trav'ling on; We are a hap-py pilgrim band, Gay-ly trav'ling on.

CHORUS.
On to the shores of the Beulah land, The happy land, the heav'nly land, On to the shores of the Beulah land, The happy Beulah land.

From "Holy Voices," by permission of E. S. Lorenz.

2 We are a little soldier band,
  Marching on, marching on ;
We are a fearless soldier band,
  Bravely marching on.

3 We are a little working band,
  Toiling on, toiling on ;

We are a busy working band,
  Gladly toiling on.

4 We are a little Christian band,
  Hoping on, praying on ;
We are an earnest Christian band,
  Hoping, praying on.

300. Little Trav'lers.

L. MASON.

1. Lit-tle trav'lers, Zi-on-ward, Each one ent'ring in-to rest, In the kingdom of your Lord, In the mansions of the blest;

There, to welcome, Jesus waits, Gives the crowns his foll'wers win; Lift your heads, ye golden gates! Let the little trav'lers in!

2 Who are they whose little feet,
  Pacing life's dark journey through,
Now have reached that heavenly seat
  They had ever kept in view?
"I from Greenland's frozen land;"
  "I from India's sultry plain;"
"I from Afric's barren sand;"
  "I from islands of the main."

3 "All our earthly journey past,
  Every tear and pain gone by,
Here together met at last,
  At the portal of the sky !
Each the welcome 'Come' awaits,
  Conqu'rors over death and sin !"
Lift your heads, ye golden gates!
  Let the little trav'lers in!

301. Take My Hand.

KATE OSBORN. WILLIAM W. BENTLEY, by per.

With feeling.

1. Ev-er bless-ed Jesus, List-en un-to me, Bow thine ear and hear me, While I call to thee;
I am weak and sin-ful, Thou art pure and strong, Take my hand, dear Je-sus, Lead thy child a-long.

CHORUS.
Take my hand, dear Je-sus, Let me nev-er stray, Take my hand and lead me In the bet-ter way.

2 Ever blessed Jesus,
Bless thy wayward child,
Keep my feet from straying
Through the desert wild;
I would never wander
From thy loving side,
Ever, blessed Jesus,
Be my constant guide.

3 Help me, blessed Jesus,
Leave me not alone,
Give me strength and patience
Till each duty's done;
And when life is ended,
I thy face would see;
Hear my prayer, dear Jesus,
Take me up to thee.

302. Jesus, Gentle Saviour.

WM. W. BENTLEY, by per.

Mildly.

1. Je-sus, gen-tle Sav-iour, Ev-er meek and mild, In thy ten-der mer-cy, Hear a lit-tle child;
Teach me how to love thee, Teach me how to pray, Whis-per to my spir-it, Tell me what to say.

2 Like a gentle shepherd,
Lead me all the day;
Saviour, do not leave me,
Let me never stray;
When my steps are weary,
Lay me on thy breast,
Sweet will be my slumber,
Peaceful there my rest.

3 With the birds that praise thee,
Singing in the shade,
And the streams rejoicing,
With all thou hast made;
Jesus, I would praise thee
In my joyful song,
Of thy loving kindness
Singing all day long.

303. Children's Prayer.

"Ye are the light of the world."—MATT. 5: 14.

M. J. MUNGER.

1. God, make my life a little light Within the world to glow, A little flame that burneth bright Wherever I may go; God, make my life a little song That comforteth the sad, That helpeth others to be strong, And make the sinner glad.

2 God, make my life a little staff
Whereon the weak may rest,
That so what health and strength I have
May serve my neighbors best;

God, make my life a little hymn
Of tenderness and praise,
Of faith that never waxeth dim
In all his wond'rous ways.

304. Children's Morning Prayer.

"Evening, and morning, and at noon, will I pray."—PSA. 55: 17.

S. C. HANSON.

1. Father, help thy little child; Make me truthful, good and mild, Kind, obedient, modest, meek, Mindful of the words I speak.

2 What is right may I pursue,
What is wrong, refuse to do,

What is evil, seek to shun,
This I ask thro' Christ the Son.

305. Jesus, Bless the Children.

E. R. LATTA.
J. H. FILLMORE.

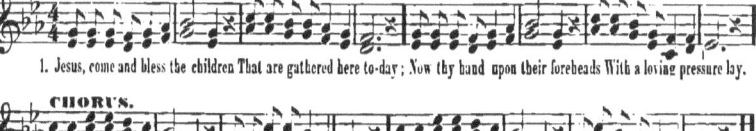

1. Jesus, come and bless the children That are gathered here to-day; Now thy hand upon their foreheads With a loving pressure lay.

CHORUS.

Jesus, come and bless the children With a blessing all divine; Shield them from the wiles of Satan, Make and keep them ever thine.

2 Jesus, come and bless the children,
Just as tenderly again,
As before thy crucifixion,
When upon the earth with men.

3 Jesus, come and bless the children,
Keep their spirits, Lord, from ill;
And upon their earthly journey,
Let them feel thy presence still.

306 Sweetly Sing, Sweetly Sing.

Miss J. W. Sampson.   Mendel.

1. Sweet-ly sing, sweet-ly sing, Prais-es to our heav'nly King; Let us raise, let us raise, High our notes of praise; Praise to him whose name is Love, Praise to him who reigns above; Raise your songs, raise your songs, Now with thankful tongues.

2 Angels bright, angels bright,
Robed in garments pure and white,
Chant his praise, chant his praise,
In melodious lays;
But from that bright, happy throng,
Ne'er can come this sweetest song—
Redeeming love, redeeming love,
Brought us here above.

3 Far away, far away,
We in sin's dark valley lay;
Jesus came, Jesus came,
Blessed be his name!

He redeemed us by his grace,
Then prepared in heaven a place
To receive — to receive
All who will believe.

4 Now we know, now we know
We to heaven must shortly go;
Soon the call, soon the call
Comes to one and all;
Saviour! when our time shall come,
Take us to our heavenly home,
There we'll raise notes of praise,
Through unending days.

307   "We are Jesus' Little Lambs."

Kate Cameron.   Harry Sanders, by per.

1. We are Je-sus' lit-tle lambs, And our Shepherd well we love; He will take us in his arms, Bear us safe to fields a-bove. Lit-tle lambs, lit-tle lambs, We have no fear, If we are in dan-ger, Je-sus is near.

2 In those pastures, green and fair,
We shall roam secure from harm,
Ever kept from grief and ill,
By our shepherd's mighty arm.

3 Let us love and trust him more,
Strive to serve him here below;
Thinking of the blessed time,
When to dwell with him we'll go.

308. Can You Tell?

1. Little schoolmates, can you tell Who has kept us safe and well, Thro' the watches of the night, Till the morning light? Yes; it is our God doth keep Little children while they sleep; He has kept us safe from harm, By his pow'rful arm.

2 Can you tell who gives us food,
Clothes, and home, and parents good,
Schoolmates dear, and teachers kind,
Books, and active mind?
2d C. Yes; our heavenly Father's care
Gives us all we eat and wear;
All our books and all our friends,
God in kindness sends.

3 *All.* O, then, let us thankful be,
For his mercies large and free;
Every morning let us raise
High our song of praise;
Praise him for these happy hours,
Praise him for our varied powers,
Praise him, every heart and voice,
While we all rejoice.

309. I Want to be Like Jesus.

L. H. D.   E. L. WHITE.

1. { I want to be like Jesus, So gentle, pure and mild;
    For if I live like Jesus, He'll own me as his child. }
I want to be his soldier As long as I shall live; Because he died to save me, My life to him I'll give.

2 I want to follow Jesus,
    I want to learn his ways,
I want to call him Master,
    I want to sing his praise.

I want to work for Jesus,
    I'll triumph in his love,
And then I'll surely know him
    In that bright home above.

310. God is Love.

HARRY LEE.   J. H. F.

1. "God is love," the snow-flakes whisper, As they lin-ger in the air; "God is love," the breez-es mur-mur,

REFRAIN.

As they meet us ev-'ry-where. God is love, God is love, All things tell us, "God is love."

2 Little stars that shine in heaven,
   As they twinkle far above,
   Peeping, smiling at each other,
   Whisper gently, "God is love."

3 "God is love," the little birdies,
   In the tree-tops overhead,

Seem to say with their sweet voices—
   Praising him, by whom they're fed.

4 Little children, too, can praise him,
   As they carol, "God is love;"
   Trusting very soon to see him,
   In the land of life above.

311. The Narrow Way.

"Because strait is the gate, and narrow is the way, which leadeth unto life."—MATT. 7:14.

Moderato.   A. J. ABBEY.

1. The way to heav'n is nar-row, And its bless-ed entrance strait, But how safe the lit-tle pil-grims Who get with-in the gate! We will take the nar-row way, We will take the nar-row way; We will fol-low Je-sus' bid-ding, And take the nar-row way.

2 The sunbeams of the morning
   Make the narrow path so fair,
   And these early little pilgrims
   Find dewy blessings there.

3 They pass o'er rugged mountains,
   But they climb them with a song,

For these early little pilgrims
   Have sandals new and strong.

4 They know it leads to heaven
   With its bright and open gates,
   Where for happy little pilgrims
   A Saviour's welcome waits.

312. Sweet Story of Old.

Mrs Luke. "He put his hands upon them, and blessed them."—Mark 10: 16. J. C. Engelbrecht.

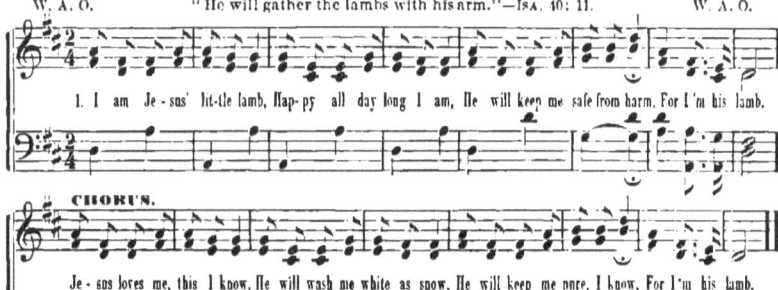

2 I wish that his hands had been placed on my head,
His arms had been thrown around me,
And that I might have seen his kind looks when he said,
Let the little ones come unto me.

Cho.—||: Let the little ones come unto me, :||
And that I might have seen his kind looks when he said,
Let the little ones come unto me.

3 Yet still to his footstool in prayer I may go,
And ask for a share in his love;
And if I thus earnestly seek him below,
I shall see him and hear him above.

Cho.—||: I shall see him and hear him above, :||
And if I thus earnestly seek him below,
I shall see him and hear him above.

313. Jesus' Little Lamb.

W. A. O. "He will gather the lambs with his arm."—Isa. 40: 11. W. A. O.

From "Crown of Life," by permission of W. W. Whitney.

2 By his staff I'm led along,
Guarded by his arm so strong,
I'm so happy all day long,
For I'm his lamb.

3 Then I never will repine,
While around his glories shine,
I am his and he is mine,
O, I'm his lamb.

314. How I Wish I Knew.

GRACE GLENN.   J. H. FILLMORE.

1. Lit-tle stars that twin-kle in the heav-ens blue, I have oft-en wondered if you ev-er knew How there rose one like you, lead-ing wise old men From the East, thro' Ju-dah, down to Beth-le-hem?

2 Did you see the costly presents they had brought?
Did you see the stable they in wonder sought?
Did you see the worship tenderly they paid
To that stranger baby in the manger laid?

3 Did you hear the mothers pleading through their tears
For the babes that Herod slew the coming years?
Did you see how Joseph, warned of God in dreams,
Hurried into Egypt, guided by your beams?

4 Did you watch the Saviour all those years of strife?
Did you know for sinners how he gave his life?
Little stars that twinkle in the heavens blue,
All you saw of Jesus, how I wish I knew.

315. Blessed Jesus.

J. H. F.

1. Who was in a man-ger laid? Je-sus, blessed Je-sus,
Who for money was betrayed? (Omit, ...) Je-sus, blessed Je-sus.
Who up Cal-va-ry was led?
Who for us his life-blood shed? Jesus Christ, creation's head, Jesus, blessed Je-sus.

2 Who can rob the grave of gloom?
  Jesus, blessed Jesus.
Who can raise us from the tomb?
  Jesus, blessed Jesus.
When before the Judge we wait,
Who will open heaven's gate?
Jesus Christ, our Advocate,
  Jesus, blessed Jesus.

3 Who will give us sweetest rest?
  Jesus, blessed Jesus.
Who, in heaven, shall we love best?
  Jesus, blessed Jesus.
At his feet our crowns we'll fling,
While with rapturous songs we sing,
Jesus Christ, our Saviour, King,
  Jesus, blessed Jesus.

316. Little Gleaners.

"I write unto you, little children, because your sins are forgiven you for his name's sake."—1 John 2: 12.

Jepson.

1. We are a bus-y glean-ing band, That can not bind the sheaves; But we can fol-low those who reap, And gath-er what each leaves. We are not strong, but Je-sus loves The weak-est of the fold; And in our fee-ble ef-forts proves His ten-der-ness un-told.

CHORUS.
We are a bus-y gleaning band, That can not bind the sheaves; But we can fol-low those who reap, And gath-er what each leaves.

2 We are not rich, but we can give,
As we are passing on,
A cup of water in his name,
To some poor fainting one.
We are not wise, but Christ, our Lord,
Revealed to babes his will;
And we are sure from his dear word,
He loves the children still.

3 We know that with our gather'd grain,
Briars and leaves are seen;
Yet, since we tried, he smiles the same,
And takes our offering.
Dear children, still hosannas sing,
As Christ doth conqu'ring come;
Casting your treasures as he brings
The heathen nations home.

317. Little Things.

1. Lit-tle drops of wa-ter, Lit-tle grains of sand, Make the mighty o-cean, And the beauteous land.
2. And the lit-tle mo-ments, Hum-ble tho' they be, Make the mighty a-ges Of e-ter-ni-ty.

3 So our little errors
Lead the soul away,
From the paths of virtue,
Oft in sin to stray.

4 Little deeds of kindness,
Little deeds of love,
Make our earth an Eden,
Like the heav'n above.

5 Little seeds of mercy,
Sown by youthful hands,
Grow to bless the nations,
Far in heathen lands.

318. The Little Hands.

T. CORBEN. BISHOP W. JOHNS.

1. Beau-ti-ful the lit-tle hands That fulfill the Lord's commands; Beautiful the little eyes, Kindled with light from the skies.

CHORUS.
Beau-ti-ful, beau-ti-ful lit-tle hands, That ful-fill the Lord's commands; Beau-ti-ful, beauti-ful lit-tle eyes, Kindled with light from the skies.

2 All the little hands were made
Jesus' precious cause to aid;
All the little hearts to beat
Warm in his service so sweet.

3 All the little lips should pray
To the Saviour every day

All the little feet should go
Swift on his errands below.

4 What your little hands can do,
That the Lord intends for you;
Make that thing your first delight,
Do it to him with your might.

319. Little Ones, Listen.

1. Lit-tle eyes, lit-tle eyes, Where are you gaz-ing? Not where sin's fires a-rise Flash-ing and blaz-ing? Look up! the soft blue sky Bend-ing en-folds you; Look up! a Fa-ther's eye Lov-ing be-holds you.
2. Lit-tle hands, lit-tle hands, What are you do-ing? Break-ing his dear com-mands, E-vil pur-su-ing; Do the sweet works of love, On-ly and ev-er; God in his heav'n a-bove Aids that en-dea-vor.

3 Little tongue, little tongue,
What are you saying?
Speak ne'er a word of wrong
Working or playing.
Speak but for love and truth —
Holy and winning;
In the sweet bloom of youth,
Heaven's song beginning.

4 Little feet, little feet,
Where are you moving?
Let not the tempter meet
Steps idly roving.
Walk where the good have trod,
Heavenward before you;
Christ's feet have pressed the sod,
He watches o'er you.

5 Little heart, little heart,
Seeking God's altar—
Choosing the better part—
O, do not falter!
Gentle, and wise, and pure,
All to him given;
Thine is the promise sure
"Written in heaven."

320. Busy Little Gleaners.

J. H. K.   "Go ye therefore into the highways."—MATT. 22:9.   J. H. KURZENKNABE.

1. Gathering in the early dawn, Gathering when the night comes on; Yonder in the ripened fields, Hundred fold the harvest yields. 1. The golden grain is gathered in, The sheaves of good from fields of sin, By busy little gleaners, By busy little gleaners.

2 Tho' reapers come from far and near,
The Master leaves an honored share
For busy little gleaners,
For busy little gleaners.

3 Out in the highway where you go,
To plant or reap, there's work to do
For busy little gleaners,
For busy little gleaners.

4 Amid the glow of autumn leaves,
We carry home our golden sheaves,
Such happy little gleaners,
Such happy little gleaners.

321. Two Little Hands.

W. A. OGDEN.

1. I've two little hands to work for Jesus, One little tongue his praise to tell, Two little ears to hear his counsel, One little voice a song to swell.

CHORUS.   1st time.   2d time.

Lord, we come, Lord, we come, In our childhood's early morning, Come to learn of thee.

2 I've two little feet to tread the pathway,
Up to the heavenly courts above;
Two little eyes to read the Bible,
Telling of Jesus' wondrous love.

3 I've one little heart to give to Jesus,
One little soul for him to save,
One little life for his dear service,
One little self that he must have.

MISCELLANEOUS.

"Thou crownest the year with thy goodness."—Ps. 65: 11.

325   Welcome to All.

C. C. CLINE.   (FOR CONVENTIONS.)   C. C. CLINE.

1. We welcome you, friends of our Master and Lord, To share in the joys which our feasts will afford;

To fill us with love for the work of our King, And help us to him greater tribute to bring.

CHORUS.   Rit.

Then a welcome to all, happy welcome to all; Thrice welcome, happy welcome, happy welcome to all.

2 We bid you a welcome to homes and to hearts
  Aglow with the friendship which Jesus imparts
  With us to rejoice in the bountiful love
  And blessings so rich from the Father above.

3 We greet you, dear brethren in Christ, with a prayer,
  That love, joy and peace may abide with us here;
  That wisdom and prudence may guide us aright
  In all that pertains to the kingdom of light.

4 At last, when our meetings and partings are o'er,
  May all find a welcome on heaven's bright shore,
  When honor and praise to our God we will sing,
  Through Jesus, our Saviour, Redeemer, and King.

Greeting Song.

JULIA A. JOHNSTON.   For Conventions.   LUCY J. RIDER, by per.

1. Welcome day of glad re-un-ion! Let its hours be filled with praise! God himself has

D. S. *In this fellow-*

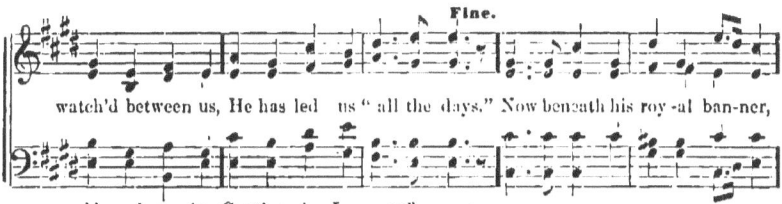

watch'd between us, He has led us "all the days." Now beneath his roy-al ban-ner,

ship and serv-ice, Greeting in Im-manuel's name.

On this vantage ground we stand, Greetings joyfully exchanging, Heart to heart and

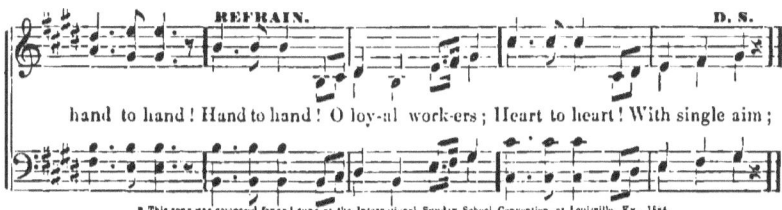

hand to hand! Hand to hand! O loy-al work-ers; Heart to heart! With single aim;

* This song was composed for and sung at the International Sunday School Convention, at Louisville, Ky., 1884.

1 Welcome! day of glad reunion!
  Let its hours be filled with praise!
 God himself has watched between us,
  He has led us "all the days."
 Now beneath his royal banner,
  On this vantage ground we stand,
 Greetings joyfully exchanging,
  Heart to heart and hand to hand!

2 In thy name, O Lord, assembled,
  We would praise and tribute bring,
 We would join our hallelujahs,
  In the honor of the King!

Thanks to him who gave the message,
  For his blessing on the word,
 "Great the company who publish,"
  Great the number who have heard.

3 While upon this mount we tarry,
  Tho' we may not build and stay,
 May we find in sweet communion,
  Strength to cheer the future way.
 When all other faces vanish,
  And these golden hours are told,
 'Twill suffice, if "Jesus only"
  We may evermore behold.

2 Hither we come, a happy throng,
Love and loyalty confessing to the reigning Prince of Peace;
Him we adore; to him belong
Glory, honor, power and blessing, and his kingdom shall increase!

3 Glory to God, who reigns above,
Father, Son and Holy Spirit, 'throned in peerless majesty!
Shout the refrain that God is love!
Let it echo! echo! echo! over every land and sea!

328 Welcome.

C. C. CLINE. (FESTIVAL OCCASIONS) Har. by C. C. CLINE.

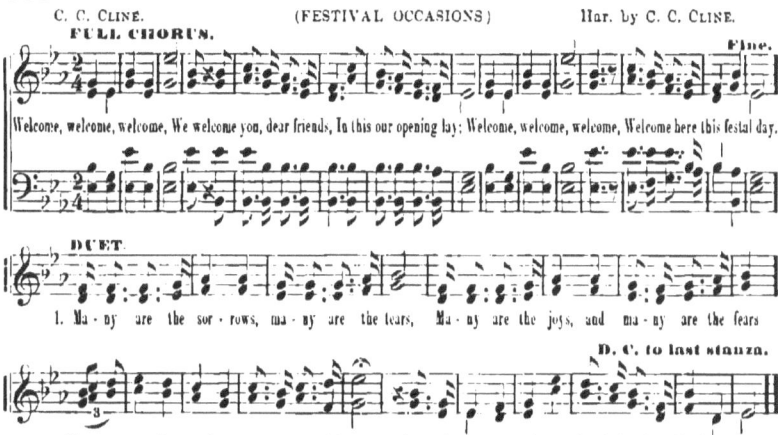

Welcome, welcome, welcome, We welcome you, dear friends, In this our opening lay; Welcome, welcome, welcome, Welcome here this festal day.

1. Ma-ny are the sor-rows, ma-ny are the tears, Ma-ny are the joys, and ma-ny are the fears That have crossed our pathway since we last did meet, But we've come a-gain, our kin-dred and our friends to greet.

2 Many are the conflicts, many are the snares,
Many are the trials, and many are the cares
That we've borne through Jesus since we last did meet,
But we're here again, our brethren and our friends to greet.

3 Many are the pleasures that we here shall share,
Many are the treasures we must homeward bear,
That we may be true till we the Master meet,
When we'll come again, our loved ones and our friends to greet.

329 Joy-Bells.

JOSEPHINE POLLARD. "Be glad and rejoice."—Ps. 9:2. HENRY TUCKER.

1. Joy-bells ringing, Children singing, Fill the air with music sweet; Jocund measure, Guileless pleasure, Make the chain of song complete.

{ Joy - bells! joy - bells! Nev-er, nev-er cease your ring-ing; }
{ Chil-dren! chil-dren! Nev-er, nev-er cease your sing-ing; } List, list, the song that swells, Joy-bells! Joy-bells!

2 Joy-bells ringing,
  Children singing,
Hark! their voices, loud and clear;
  Breaking o'er us,
  Like a chorus,
From a purer, happier sphere.

3 Earth seems brighter,
  Hearts grow lighter,
As the jocund melody
  Charms our sadness
  Into gladness,
Pealing, pealing joyfully

4 Joy-bells nearer
  Sound, and clearer,
When the heart is free from care;
  Skies are cheering,
  And we're hearing
Joy-bells ringing everywhere.

331   Glory be to God.

FRANK M. DAVIS.

1 Glory to God in the highest,
  Legions of angels do cry,
  Christ for his people has risen,
  With him they'll triumph on high.

2 Faintly one heard the sweet voices,
  Filling the dome of the sky,
  Glory to God in the highest,
  Glory to God the most high.

Christmas Bells.

2 The bells—the merry Christmas bells!
   They're ringing in the morn;
 They ring when in the eastern sky
   The golden light is born;
 They ring as sunshine tips the hills
   And gilds the glittering spire;
 When through the sky the sovereign sun
   Rolls his full orb of fire.

3 The bells—the silvery Christmas bells!
   O'er many a mile they sound;
 And household tones are answering them
   In thousand homes around.
 Let childhood's voices, blithe and shrill,
   With youth's strong accents blend;
 Let every thoughtful human heart
   In praise to God ascend.

Happy Christmas Time.

H. S. PERKINS. WILLIAM W. BENTLEY, by per.

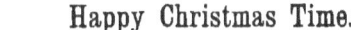

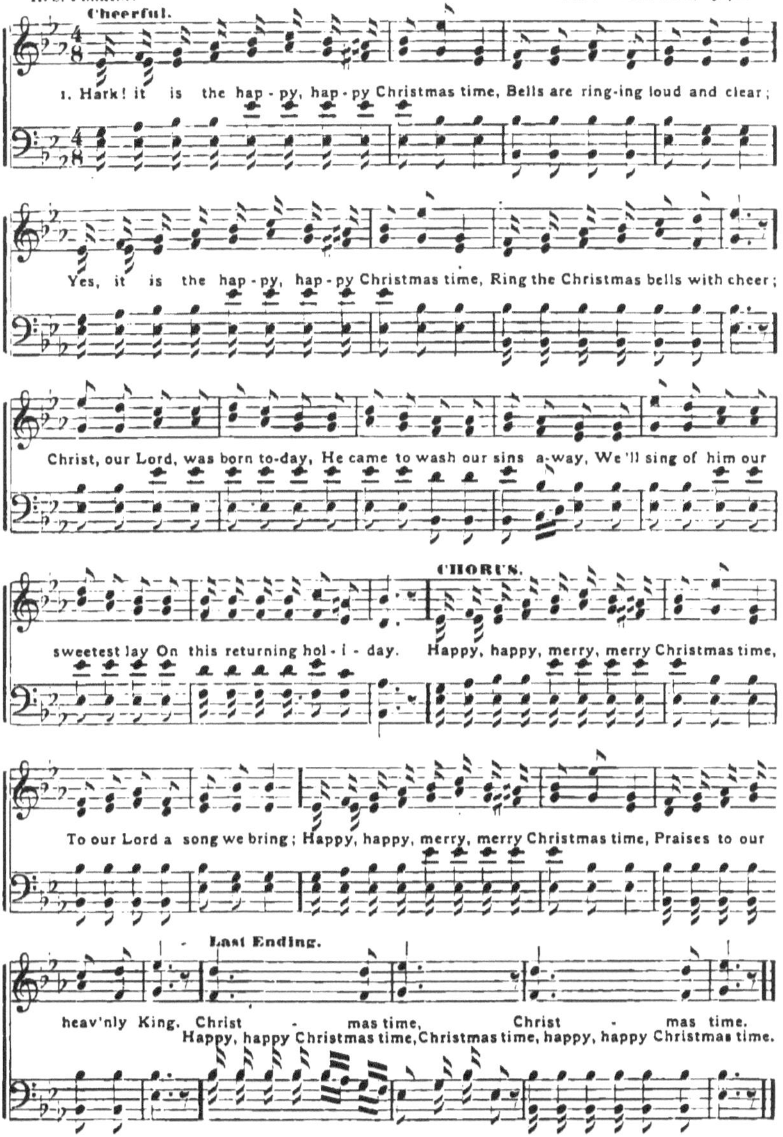
Cheerful.
1. Hark! it is the hap-py, hap-py Christmas time, Bells are ring-ing loud and clear;
Yes, it is the hap-py, hap-py Christmas time, Ring the Christmas bells with cheer;
Christ, our Lord, was born to-day, He came to wash our sins a-way, We'll sing of him our
sweetest lay On this returning hol-i-day.
CHORUS.
Happy, happy, merry, merry Christmas time,
To our Lord a song we bring; Happy, happy, merry, merry Christmas time, Praises to our
Last Ending.
heav'nly King. Christ - mas time, Christ - mas time.
Happy, happy Christmas time, Christmas time, happy, happy Christmas time.

2 We will join the happy, happy Christmas time,
With our voices full and strong;
'Tis the day that ev'ry happy voice should chime
With a cheerful hymn and song;
For our Lord is King of kings,
His coming full salvation brings,
Earth with its hallelujah rings,
And ev'ry holy angel sings.

334. A Christmas Hymn.

ELEANOR A. HUNTER.
REV. GEO. VOLES.

From ev'ry spire on Christmas Eve, The Christmas bells ring clearly out Their message of good-will and peace With many a call and silver shout. For faithful hearts, the angels' song Still echoes in the frosty air, And by the altar low they bow, In ad-o-ra-tion and in prayer.

2 A thousand blessed mem'ries throng,
 The stars are holy signs to them,
And from the eyes of ev'ry child
 Looks forth the babe of Bethlehem;
But there are others, not like these,
 Whose brows are sad, whose hopes are cross'd.
To whom the season brings no cheer,
 And life's most gracious charm is lost.

2 To whom that story, old and sweet,
 Is but a fable at the best,
The Christmas music mocks their ears,
 And life has naught of joy or rest.

Oh! for an angel's voice to pierce
 The clouds of grief that o'er them rise,
The mists of doubt and unbelief,
 That veil the blue of Christmas skies.

4 That they, at last, may see the light
 Which shines from Bethlehem, and unfold
For Christ the treasures of their hearts,
 Richer than spicery or gold.
Hope of the ages, draw thou near,
 'Till all the earth shall own thy sway,
And when thou reign'st in ev'ry heart
 It will, indeed, be Christmas day.

335. Autumn Leaves.

WM. WALSHAM HOW.
FREDERICK ILIFFE.

The year is swiftly wan-ing, The summer days are past; And life, brief life, is speed-ing: The end is nearing fast.

2 The ever-changing seasons
 In silence come and go;
But thou, Eternal Father,
 No time or change canst know.

3 Oh! pour thy grace upon us
 That we may worthier be,

Each year that passes o'er us,
 To dwell in heaven with thee.

4 Our barren hearts make fruitful
 With every goodly grace,
That we thy name may hallow,
 And see at last thy face.

Wake the Song of Jubilee. Concluded.

338. Children's Song of Praise.
MRS. R. N. TURNER.   WM. J. KIRKPATRICK.

1. Strains of music rising To the courts above, Bear our praises upward To the Lord of love! Tribute glad we're bringing, At his feet to lay, Joyful songs we're singing On this happy day! Praise him, praise him, Ev'ry youthful heart! Birds and buds and blossoms Gladly do their part! Praise him, praise him, Ev'ry youthful heart! Birds and buds and blossoms gladly do their part.

Copyright, 1890, by Wm. J. Kirkpatrick.

2 Fragrant flowers are springing
At his blest command,
All their grace receiving,
From his loving hand!
In this glory sharing,
Let us hasten now,
Crowns of beauty bearing,
To adorn his brow!

3 With our festal gladness,
Every eye is bright,
With our Father's blessing
Every heart is light!
Then with eager voices,
Raise the song above,
While each heart rejoices,
In the Lord we love!

339. Praise ye the Lord.

"Let everything that hath breath praise the Lord."—Ps. 150 : 6.

L. H. P.   L. H. PARTHMORE.

1. Praise ye the Lord, praise him with songs of gladness, Come unto him, bringing your cares and sadness;
He's our Saviour, God, and King, He hath redeemed us, from sin redeemed us, Bought our pardon on the cross, and set us free. O then praise the Lord; Yes, praise his name, His wondrous works a-broad proclaim; Swell, swell the song, from shore to shore, O glory be un-to the Lord for evermore.

2 Praise ye the Lord, praise him ye saints in glory,
   Angels above tell of the wondrous story,
  How for man he came to die,
  He who is worthy, alone is worthy;
  Glory be unto his name—the mighty King!

3 Praise ye the Lord, praise ye him ev'ry nation;
   Sing to his name, sing to him all creation;
  He's our strong and mighty tower,
  He is our Saviour, our strong deliv'rer;
  Praise and honor be to God for evermore.

340. Roll the Chorus of Praise Along.

"To whom be praise and dominion forever and ever."—1 Pet. 4: 11.

CHARLOTTE ABBEY.   FRANK M. DAVIS, by per.

1. The day of Ju-bi-lee is come; Let ev-'ry heart rejoice, and sing
2. With mer-cies he has crowned the year, Our steps has guarded all the way;
3. We sing in loud and joy-ous strain The glo-ry, hon-or, of our King,

Sweet prais-es to our ris-en Lord; Let earth with hal-le-lu-jahs ring.
O laud and mag-ni-fy his name This joy-ful An-ni-vers'-ry day.
While saints and an-gels swell the song, And make the heavenly arch-es ring.

CHORUS.

Then roll the cho-rus of praise a-long; Let earth re-
Then roll the cho - - - rus of praise a-long; Let earth re-

ech-o the joy-ful song; The Lord is King of the
ech - - - o the song, joy-ful song; The Lord is King

earth and sky; E-ter-nal is his throne on high.
of the earth and sky; E-ter - - nal is his throne on high.

342. A New-Year's Greeting.

E. L. White.

1 Come, children, and join in our festival song,
   The new year has come, and the old year has gone;
   We'll join our glad voices in one hymn of praise
   To God, who has kept us and lengthened our days.

2 Our Father in heaven, we lift up to thee
   Our voice of thanksgiving, our glad jubilee;
   Oh, bless us, and guide us, dear Saviour, we pray,
   That from thy blest precepts we never may stray.

3 And if, ere this New Year has drawn to a close,
   Some loved one among us in death shall repose,
   Grant, Lord, that the spirit in heaven may dwell,
   In the bosom of Jesus, where all shall be well.

4 Kind teachers, we children would thank you this day,
   That faithfully, kindly, you've taught us the way
   How we may escape from the world's sinful charms,
   And find a safe refuge in the Saviour's loved arms.

5 Dear Pastor, we ask thee, as lambs of thy fold,
   To teach us that wisdom more precious than gold—
   Our footsteps to guide in the pathway of truth,
   To "love our Creator in the days of our youth."

6 And now, as we enter another New Year,
   We pray for a blessing on your labors here;
   May many "bright jewels" be your blest reward,
   And "crowns of rejoicing in the day of the Lord."

343. Good-Night.

ELLA LANDER. D. B. TOWNER.

1 Loving word that's nightly whisper'd
  O'er each tiny trundle-bed,
  While a mother's benediction
  Falls upon the sleeper's head.

2 When the toils of day are over,
  Friend to friend bids soft good-night,
  Praying that the coming morrow
  Be with heaven's blessing bright.

3 Gently whisper'd by the dying,
  At the fading of the day:
  Ent'ring in upon the shining
  Of the heav'nly light for aye.

4 Some good-night will be the last one,
  When our days of earth are o'er,
  When we reach the shining portal
  And earth's twilights are no more.

INDEX OF TITLES AND FIRST LINES.

Titles in SMALL CAPS; First lines in Roman; Figures indicate Nos. of Hymns

As forth from the city went Jesus one day	26
ARE THERE TEN TO-DAY,	35
All praise to Jesus' hallowed name,	67
A FRIEND THAT'S EVER NEAR,	83
A BLESSING IN PRAYER.	87
All glory to Jesus be given,	98
A Christian band from far and near,	106
ALL AROUND THE WORLD,	118
A Lord's Day well spent,	125
AWAY WITH THE RUBY WINE,	187
ANGRY WORDS,	188
At the sounding of the trumpet,	217
Around the throne of God in heaven,	254
After the voyage and the water's mad riot	261
A dear little army of children,	275
ALLELICA! SWEETLY SING.	279
All is bright and cheerful round us,	279
ALL THE WAY,	283
A CHRISTMAS HYMN,	334
AUTUMN LEAVES.	335
A HAPPY NEW YEAR,	341
Another bright year has flitted away,	341
A New Year's Greeting,	342
BRIGHTEST AND BEST,	7
BEAUTIFUL STAR IN THE EAST,	8
BECAUSE HE LOVED ME SO,	14
BLUE SEA OF GALILEE,	22
BLIND BARTIMEUS,	26
BEHOLD THE LAMB,	41
Blessed morn of light and glory,	42
Blessed be the name of Christ, our Savior	69
BEAUTIFUL SONGS.	73
BLESSED WORDS,	102
BOOK OF GRACE,	167
BEAUTIFUL WATER,	183
Be not swift to take offense,	194
BE KIND TO THE LOVED ONES AT HOME,	201
BUDS OF PROMISE,	223
Blooming all for Jesus,	223
BEAUTIFUL THINGS,	227
Beautiful ground on which we tread,	227
BEAUTIFUL HOME,	242
BEYOND THE SUNSET,	244
Beautiful realm of delight,	246
Beyond the smiling and the weeping	250
BY AND BYE,	253
BEAUTIFUL THE LITTLE HANDS	287
BLESS US AND KEEP US,	288
BLESSED JESUS,	315
Beautiful the little hands,	318
BUSY LITTLE GLEANERS,	320
CONDESCENSION,	10
Christ is merciful and mild,	10
Come down beside the waters,	21
CROSS OF JESUS,	40
CHRIST AROSE,	44
Christ, above all glory seated,	43
Come, children, and join in our festival song,	74
COME WITH CHEERFUL SINGING,	82
CROSS OF JESUS,	55
Cross of Jesus—blessed symbol,	55
CHILDREN'S TE DEUM,	88
Children, when you sing and pray,	95
COME AND HEAR THE STORY TOLD,	108
CLEAVE TO THE SAVIOUR,	119
Children, would you know the story,	164
Come unto me, whoever is thirsty,	168
Come, let us sing of fount and spring,	178
CHILD OF THE DRUNKARD,	179
CAST DOWN THE CUP,	181
CATCH THE SUNSHINE.	226
COME AWAY TO THE S. S.	270
COME TO SUNDAY SCHOOL,	278
Come, while the grass in the path we tread,	278
CHRISTMAS MORNING,	286
CHILDREN'S PRAYER.	303
CHILDREN'S MORNING PRAYER,	304
CAN YOU TELL,	308
CHRISTMAS BELLS,	332
CHILDREN'S SONG OF PRAISE,	333
Come, children, and join in our festival song,	342
DO SOMETHING TO-DAY,	109
Down in the valley with my Saviour I would go,	124
DRINK AND LIVE,	168
DARE TO DO RIGHT,	177
DOWN IN A DELL,	184
Do you slumber in your tent, Christian soldier,	199
DON'T FORGET THE OLD FOLKS,	208
Each cooing dove and sighing bough,	23, 32
Eternal Father, thou hast said,	116
Ever blessed Jesus,	301
From all the dark places,	121
FREE GIVING,	131
FOLLOW ME,	140
FOLLOW THOU ME,	143
FOLLOWING JESUS,	144
FADING FLOWER,	243
FRIEND OF CHILDREN, HEAR,	293
Father, help thy little child,	304
From every spire on Christmas eve,	334
FOLLOW ON,	124
Guard, my child, thy tongue,	189
Gushing so bright in the morning light,	203
GOD WANTS THE BOYS AND GIRLS,	213
GOD IS EVER GOOD,	233
GOOD TIDINGS OF GREAT JOY,	3
Glory to God,	11
GALILEE,	32
GO, GATHER THE GOLDEN GRAIN,	31
GIVE ME JESUS,	71
Glory and praise and honor,	79
Go, spread the joyful tidings,	123
GATHER THEM INTO THE FOLD,	129
GOD SPEED THE RIGHT,	130
GATHER THEM IN,	135, 272
GROWING UP FOR JESUS,	146
GIVE ME THE BIBLE,	160

INDEX OF TITLES AND FIRST LINES.

God Make my Life a Little Light,	303
God is Love,	310
Gathering in the early dawn,	320
Greeting Song,	326
Gladly We Hail this Festal Day,	327
Glory to God! Peace on Earth,	331
Good Night,	343
Hail to the brightness of Zion's glad morning,	7
Hark to the Wondrous Music,	13
He Came for Me,	15
Hear how a sower once,	27
Hear the master calling,	29
He was Despised,	37
Hallelujah! "He is Risen,"	42, 43
He is Risen,	45
Hallelujah! He Arose,	46
He is just the same to-day,	53
Have you ever heard the story,	53
Ho, every one that thirsteth,	58
Her sad vigil keeping,	34
Happy Greeting,	74
He Loved You and Me,	80
Hark the voice of countless thousands singing,	84
Hear the royal proclamation,	97
His Love,	123
Hark the voice of Jesus calling,	126
Hark! the voice of Jesus calling,	140
How to Win,	151
Haste to the Rescue,	186
Hark! what cry arrests mine ear,	186
Honor Bright,	196
Help a Little,	204
Have You Counted the Cost, My Boy,	205
Help the Drinking Man,	206
Have you had a kindness shown,	215
Hark the lilies whisper,	232
Have you heard of the land where the ransomed dwell,	246
Home,	250
He's Watching o'er Me,	258
Hear the cheerful morning bells, calling us to Sunday-school	270
Helmet on and sword in hand,	294
Happy Beulah Land,	299
How I Wish I Knew,	314
Happy Christmas Time,	333
Hark, it is the happy, happy Christmas time,	333
Harvest Time,	113
He that goeth forth with weeping,	113
In a Manger,	9
In the holy hush of twilight,	9
I love to hear the story,	14
In the vineyard of the Master,	16
It is I, Be not Afraid,	19
I've found a friend in Jesus,	30
In the dim and early morning,	45
I will Sing with Joy,	65
I will lift my voice in a song of praise,	65
I Ought to Love my Saviour,	66
I Will Tell Jesus,	68
I've a dear Saviour, ready to listen,	68
In the Sunday-school army our names are enrolled,	80
In the ark most holy,	85
I'll Sing the Praise of Jesus,	89
I will Praise the Lord To-day,	90
I will Sing for Jesus,	91

If you have a pleasant thought,	94
I will Trust in my Saviour,	100
I want to be a Worker,	110
I Never will Leave Thee,	120
In this world of sin and woe,	122
In the desert days of old,	131
If I, like Galilee fishers,	144
If you feel a love for sinners,	151
I never open the precious book,	155
In the blessed Bible,	164
In this world of burden bearing,	204
It may be far, it may be near,	253
I Have a Sweet Hope,	259
I am Waiting,	260
In the Harbor,	261
Is it Written There,	263
I do not ask for the pride of earth,	263
I am dwelling on the mountain,	264
I will Follow Thee,	282
I washed my hands this morning,	292
I am a little soldier,	297
I Want to be like Jesus,	309
I am Jesus' little lamb,	313
I think when I read that sweet story of old,	312
I've two little hands to work for Jesus,	321
Jesus my Saviour in Bethlehem came,	15
Jesus in the Vessel,	21
Jesus in Gethsemane,	36
Jesus is Risen,	49
Jesus has burst from the fetters that bound him,	49
Jesus Lives,	50
Jesus is King,	86
Jesus, I will follow thee,	282
Jesus Bids us Shine,	291
Jesus, Gentle Saviour,	302
Jesus, Bless the Children,	305
Joy Bells,	329
Kind Words are Always best,	190
Kind Words can never Die,	192
Kneeling by her little bedside,	289
Lo, the lilies of the field,	20
Liken the kingdom to the springing,	25
Low in the grave he lay, Jesus my Saviour,	44
Lift up, O Little Children,	48
Life is full of happiness,	77
Let us meet at early dawn,	88
Let Us Sing,	93
Let Us Work,	115
Let Them Come,	133
Lambs of Jesus,	145
Looking to Jesus,	176
Like a soldier brave, his land to save,	182
Let it Pass,	194
Let us be tender, and trusty, and true,	195
Let Us Arise,	199
Love at Home,	202
Love is Kind,	215
Land of the Blessed,	248
Loving Each Other,	242
Little by Little,	276
Little Pilgrims,	85
Little children, can you tell,	286
Little Soldiers,	290
Little Feet, be Careful,	292
Looking unto Jesus,	294
Little Travelers,	300

INDEX OF TITLES AND FIRST LINES.

LITTLE SCHOOLMATES, CAN YOU TELL,	308
Little stars that twinkle in the heavens blue,	314
LITTLE GLEANERS,	316
LITTLE THINGS,	317
Little drops of water,	317
LITTLE ONES, LISTEN,	319
Little eyes, little eyes,	319
Loving word that's nightly whispered,	343
Messiah comes! the mighty Saviour,	12
MEMORIES OF GALILEE,	23
MORNING HYMN,	75
MEET ME THERE,	255
My faith to the land of the blest,	262
MUST JESUS BEAR THE CROSS?	56
Must Jesus bear the cross alone?	56
NO ONE LIKE JESUS,	76
Now, Hosanna, Son of David,	86
Now to heaven our prayers ascending,	130
'NEATH ELIM'S COOLING PALMS,	245
NOW I LAY ME DOWN TO SLEEP,	289
O WATCHING STARS, REJOICE,	11
O'er the ocean, dark and gloomy,	21
O wondrous sea of Galilee,	22
Once a feast was made, and a board was laid,	33
ON THE CROSS,	38
Oh, the gospel story tell,	39
OUT OF THE SHADOW,	51
ONCE AGAIN,	54
Once again I want to hear it,	54
Oh, the unsearchable riches of Christ,	68
Oh, sing the power of love divine,	81
O Jesus, I never will leave thee,	120
ONLY A BEAM OF SUNSHINE,	128
Open the door for the children,	129
On what are you building, my brother,	134
O never be weary, with vigor pursue,	148
Oh, the blessed word of God,	162
Oh, speak kind words where'er you be,	190
ONLY A PENNY A PIECE,	200
Oh, how sorrowful the picture,	206
Oh, be warned of your danger, nor slight the day of grace,	212
Once he sat upon my knee,	214
OH, WHAT CAN YOU TELL,	221
Over the river the crystal stream flows,	241
Oh! land of the blessed, thy shadowless skies,	248
Oh, the years they are gliding away,	251
On the happy golden shore,	255
Oh, do not be discouraged,	271
OH, COME, COME AWAY,	277
OH, COME, LITTLE CHILDREN,	281
OUR HEAVENLY GUIDE,	284
Oh, guide to richest treasures,	284
PEACE, BE STILL,	17
PRAISE TO JESUS,	67
PRAISE HIM,	77
PRAISE! GIVE PRAISE,	78
Praise him! praise him, Jesus, our blessed Redeemer,	78
PRECIOUS WORDS,	159
Precious forever, O, wonderful words,	159
PRECIOUS BIBLE,	161
Poor child of the drunkard, none careth for thee,	179
PLEASANT WEATHER,	230
PATMOS,	254
PRAISE THE LORD,	336
PRAISE YE THE LORD,	339
Rise in thy splendor, O star of the morn,	1
Rocked upon the raging billow,	17
RING THE BELLS,	47
REVIVE US AGAIN,	72
Repeat the sweet story of Jesus to me,	135
REMEMBER, JESUS LEADS,	136
RALLY FOR THE RIGHT BOYS,	182
RIFTED CLOUDS,	193
Ride not the steeds of sin, my boy,	210
RIGHT MEN ARE WANTED,	211
RING OUT, O BELLS,	330
ROLL THE CHORUS OF PRAISE ALONG,	340
STAR OF THE MORNING,	1
SILENT NIGHT,	4
Softly the night is falling,	13
See him in the garden lone,	36
STORY OF THE CROSS,	39
SINFUL CITIES,	57
SINGING FOR JESUS,	92
SINGING FROM THE HEART,	94
SING OF JESUS, SING FOREVER,	99
SWEET IT IS TO KNOW,	101
SOMETHING TO DO,	111
See the flag of Jesus,	118
Suffer little children to come unto me,	132
SATAN THE SEED IS SOWING,	147
SOWING AND REAPING,	149
Sowing in the morning, sowing seeds of kindness,	149
SEARCHING THE SCRIPTURES,	169
SPEAK GENTLY TO THE LOVING ONES,	191
SCATTER SMILES AS YOU GO,	193
Say, who hath sorrow, contentions and woe,	209
SAVE THE BOY,	214
SEE THE SNOW COME DOWN,	228
SONG OF THE LILIES,	232
See the shining dew drops,	233
See, Israel's Gentle Shepherd Stands,	
Safely through another year,	288
SAILING O'ER THE SEA,	295
SWEETLY SING, SWEETLY SING,	306
SWEET STORY OF OLD,	312
Strains of music rising,	338
THE SHEPHERDS OF BETHLEHEM,	2
They were watching on the hillsides,	2
THE KING IN THE MANGER,	5
There's a song in the air,	5
There's a star in the East,	8
THE BARREN FIG TREE,	16
There's a light on the dark and surging deep,	18
THE LILIES OF THE FIELD,	20
THY WILL BE DONE,	24
THE MUSTARD SEED,	25
THE SOWER,	27
THE VINEYARD GATE,	28
THE VINEYARD CALL,	29
The Master stood at the vineyard gate,	28
THE LILY OF THE VALLEY,	30
THE MARRIAGE OF THE KING'S SON,	33
THE MASTER CALLETH FOR THEE,	34
There were ten who stood as the Lord passed by,	35
Three hours the earth is filled with gloom,	46
THE LAMB OF CALVARY,	52

INDEX OF TITLES AND FIRST LINES.

There was love, deep love, in the cross displayed,	52
Thou Bethsaida, the lovely, down beside the sea,	57
TELL THE JOYFUL TIDINGS,	69
TELL ME ALL ABOUT JESUS,	70
Take the world, but give me Jesus,	71
The morning bright with rosy light,	75
The precious love of Jesus,	81
Tho' the days are dark with trouble,	83
There is rest, sweet rest, at the Master's feet,	87
THE ROYAL PROCLAMATION,	97
Tho' the shadows gather o'er my pathway here,	100
THE WHOLE WIDE WORLD,	105
THE ENDEAVOR BAND,	106
There's work for the hand,	111
THERE'S MUCH WE CAN DO,	114
THE BATTLE HYMN OF MISSIONS,	116
THIS LOST WORLD FOR JESUS,	117
THE SAVIOUR'S COMING,	121
THE LORD'S DAY,	125
THE ROCK AND THE SAND,	134
THE SWEET STORY,	135
THEN HOIST THE SAILS,	137
TRIUMPH BYE-AND-BYE,	150
The prize is set before us,	150
THE WONDERFUL WORD,	155
THE BLESSED BOOK,	156
There's a book which surpasses the sages,	156
THE GOLDEN RULE,	157
THE LIVING WATER,	158
There's a light in the Bible,	165
TREASURES,	166
THANK GOD FOR THE BIBLE,	170
THE SWEETEST DRAUGHT,	178
THE DRUNKARD'S WOE,	180
There's an adder in the cup,	181
TENDER, AND TRUSTY, AND TRUE,	195
There is rarely a day so sunny,	198
There is beauty all around,	202
THE SPARKLING RILL,	203
There's an amber hue in the sparkling draught,	205
TOUCH NOT THE CUP,	207
TOUCH NOT,	209
THE STEEDS OF SIN,	210
THE WINE CUP,	212
The sun is rising o'er the ocean, The smiling waters greet the day,	220
TWILIGHT IS FALLING,	221
'T IS SUMMER TIME,	222
The gentle winds are blowing,	222
Thank God for pleasant weather,	230
The winter is coming, is coming,	231
THE CRYSTAL STREAM,	241
There is a home eternal,	242
THE BEAUTIFUL SHORE,	249
There's a home for the blest on the beautiful shore,	249
THE JASPER SEA,	250
They are waiting, waiting for us,	256
THE GREAT BYE-AND-BYE,	251
THE HOPE OF THE SOUL,	252
The soul hath a hope ever dear,	252
There are little children singing 'round the throne,	256
THEY ARE GOING DOWN THE VALLEY,	257
The Saviour is watching by night and by day,	258
THE LAND OF BEULAH,	264
THERE IS A HAPPY LAND,	265
THE SUNDAY-SCHOOL ARMY,	271
THIS GRAND LITTLE ARMY,	274
This is the motto we all would obey,	275
Thou who once with man didst dwell,	293
THOU ART MY SHEPHERD,	296
THE BIBLE SAYS I MAY,	297
TAKE MY HAND,	301
THE NARROW WAY,	311
The way to heaven is narrow,	311
TWO LITTLE HANDS,	321
The bells, the bells, the Christmas bells,	332
The year is swiftly waning,	335
The day of Jubilee is come,	340
UNSEARCHABLE RICHES,	58
While shepherds watched their flocks by night,	3
WHO IS THIS?	6
WHO AMONG THE MIGHTY,	12
WALKING THE SEA,	18
When the storm in its fury on Galilee fell,	19
We praise thee, O God! for the son of thy love,	72
Who is like Jesus faithful and true,	76
WORTHY IS THE LAMB,	84, 90
WELCOME, JESUS, WELCOME,	85
WORSHIP IN SPIRIT,	95
WELCOME,	107
We welcome you, friends, to our meeting to-night,	107
WHAT CAN I DO FOR JESUS,	112
WOULD YOU PLEASE AND HONOR JESUS,	119
WORK AND PRAY,	122
WORKERS AT HOME,	126
WE'LL GATHER THEM IN,	127
What vessel are you sailing in,	137
We're coming, dear Saviour,	139
WE ARE COMING,	141
WORK SONG,	142
Work for the night is coming,	142
We are the lambs and Jesus is our shepherd,	145
WE SHALL REAP BYE-AND-BYE,	148
What can sweetly fill my soul,	158
WONDERFUL WORDS FOR ALL,	163
We bring no glittering treasures,	166
We are searching the Scriptures,	169
WE'LL CROWN THEM,	175
We'll take up our stand for the youth of our land,	175
Who hath woe and bitter sighing,	180
WATER IS BEST,	185
WHAT MAKES US HAPPY,	197
Why are we all so happy,	197
WELCOME TO MORNING,	220
WAKE THE MORNING,	225
WHY DO THE LOVELY FLOWERS BLOOM,	229
WINTER IS COMING,	231
WALKING THE GOLDEN STREETS,	240
Who, who art these clothed in garments pure and white,	240
When blooming youth is snatched away,	243
We are floating onward, hand in hand,	245
WHAT A GATHERING THAT WILL BE,	247
WATCHING FOR ME,	262
WHEN THE MORNING LIGHT,	273
We're a little pilgrim band,	285
We are little travelers, marching, marching,	290
WISE COUNSEL,	189

INDEX OF TITLES AND FIRST LINES.

We're a happy pilgrim band, 295	Wake the Song of Jubilee, 27
We are Marching, 298	
We are a little pilgrim band, 299	Unsearchable Riches. 6
"We are Jesus' Little Lambs," 307	
Who was in a manger laid? 315	Valens, 7
We are a busy gleaning band, 316	
Welcome to All, 325	Yes, Jesus is Mighty to Save, 9
We welcome you friends of our Master and Lord, 325	You're longing to work for your Master, 10
Welcome day of glad reunion, 326	Ye followers of Christ go forth, 18
Welcome, 328	Yield not to temptation, 176

www.ingramcontent.com/pod-product-compliance
Lightning Source LLC
Chambersburg PA
CBHW031830230426
43669CB00009B/1295